YOUR FATE IS IN YOUR HAND

YOUR FATE IS IN YOUR HAND

By

JOSEF RANALD

Illustrated with Cuts of Hands of Famous People

THE REILLY & LEE CO.
PUBLISHERS . . CHICAGO

YOUR FATE IS IN YOUR HAND

COPYRIGHT 1935 :: BY
THE REILLY & LEE CO.
PRINTED IN U. S. A.

CONTENTS

CHAPTER	PAGE
I. Types of Hands	11
II. The Thumb, Fingers and Nails	17
III. The General Principles of Chiromancy	22
IV. The Principal Lines of the Hand	28

FAMOUS HANDS:

ROOSEVELT	47	DARROW	69
MUSSOLINI	48	ALFONSO XIII	70
PRINCE OF WALES	49	CHARLEY CHAPLIN	71
HITLER	50	GEORGE ARLISS	72
MAC DONALD	51	PADEREWSKI	73
POPE PIUS XI	52	DE VALERA	74
GRETA GARBO	53	JANE ADDAMS	75
JOHN BARRYMORE	54	BLERIOT	76
AMELIA EARHART	55	KING ALBERT OF BELGIUM	77
VON HINDENBURG	56	MUSTAPHA KEMEL	78
BYRD	57	CHARLES G. DAWES	79
EINSTEIN	58	DOUGLAS FAIRBANKS	80
MARLENE DIETRICH	59	D' ANNUNZIO	81
BERNARD SHAW	60	EVANGELINE BOOTH	82
ROCKEFELLER	61	MME. CURIE	83
LINDBERGH	62	MARCONI	84
MARY PICKFORD	63	CALLES	85
BOBBY JONES	64	VICKI BAUM	86
HENRY FORD	65	WINSTON CHURCHILL	87
HELEN KELLER	66	ZAMORA	88
STALIN	67	ALFRED E. SMITH	89
PERSHING	68	GANDHI	90

(*Continued*)

CONTENTS — (Continued)

KING CAROL II	91
HOOVER	92
HELEN WILLS MOODY	93
MME. LUPESCU	94
H. G. WELLS	95
JACK DEMPSEY	96
MACHADO	97
LIONEL BARRYMORE	98
JOAN CRAWFORD	99
SINCLAIR LEWIS	100
CLARK GABLE	101
LADY ASTOR	102
LORD READING	103
WILLIAM E. BORAH	104
POINCARE	105
CHEVALIER	106
FANNIE HURST	107
SIR HUBERT WILKINS	108
LENORE ULRIC	109
MATA-HARI	110
WALTER DAMROSCH	111
GEORGE GERSHWIN	112
LILY PONS	113
JACKIE COOPER	114
ELISSA LANDI	115
KIPLING	116
BABE RUTH	117
GORKY	118
GENE TUNNEY	119
TROTSKY	120
KATE SMITH	121
OLIVER LODGE	122
W. T. TILDEN II	123
JANET GAYNOR	124
AIMEE McPHERSON	125
GRAND DUCHESS ANASTASIA	126
MAE WEST	127
MARIE DRESSLER	128
NAZIMOVA	129
NORMA SHEARER	130
BERTRAND RUSSELL	131
TOSCANINI	132
TAGORE	133
MRS. CALVIN COOLIDGE	134
PEGGY JOYCE	135
SIGMUND FREUD	136
ANDREW MELLON	137
ROY CHAPMAN ANDREWS	138
DINO GRANDI	139
GEN. SMUTS	140
SIGRID UNDSET	141
ZARO AGHA	142
KRISHNAMURTI	143
MARIA JERITZA	144
RUDY VALLEE	145
ABD-EL-KRIM	146

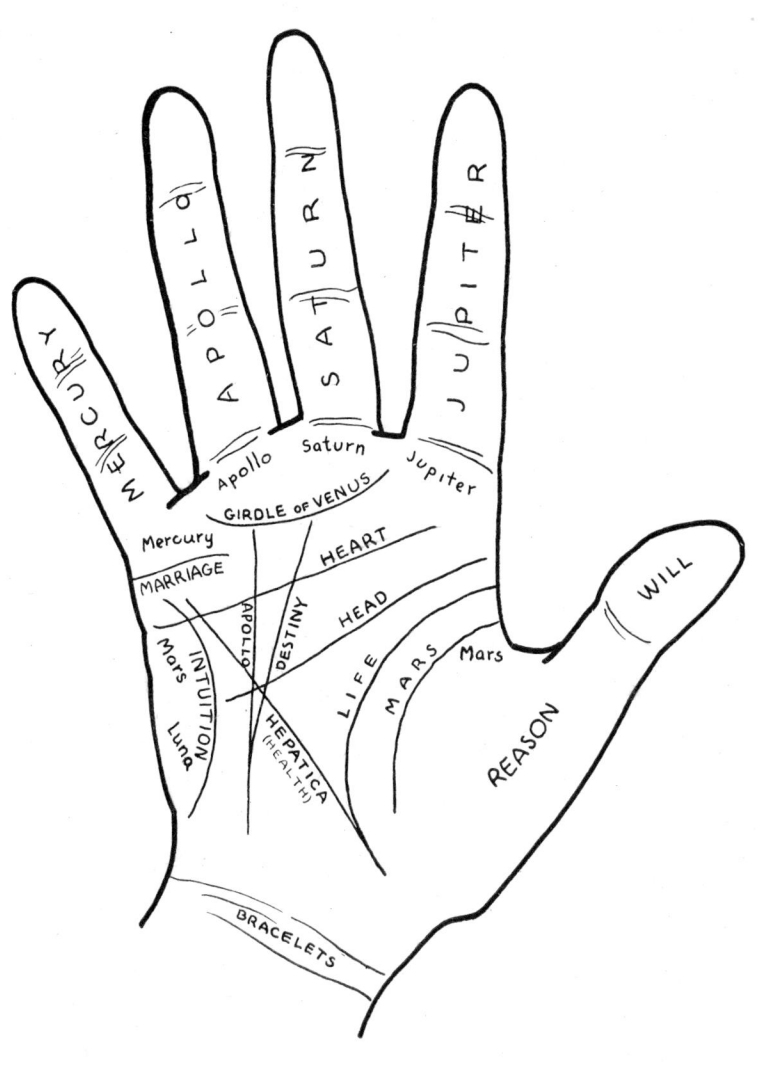

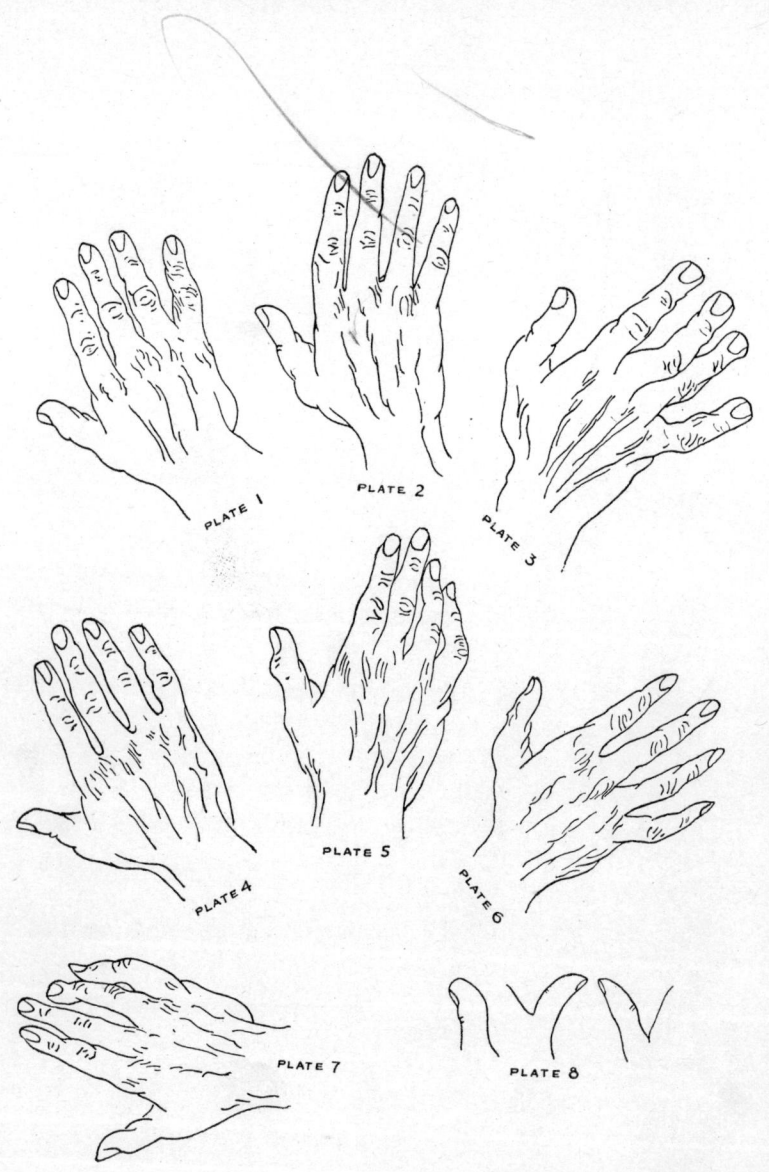

CHAPTER I

Types of Hands

Psychologists and physiologists the world over agree that, along with the convolutions of the brain, the hand and the lines in the palm serve as an index to the personality of the individual. A careful study by scientists through the centuries has led to the conclusion that the left hand serves to indicate cultural and mental inheritance, while the right hand manifests accomplishment and mental development.

In this book it is my intention to present to the reader a general view of the science of hand analysis, showing what may be gained from this fascinating study; the uses to which it may be put; the various lines indicating character, personality, talent, important events of the past and probable events of the future. Thus I wish to awaken an interest in this subject that will lead to a more exhaustive investigation. In the accompanying reproductions of the lines of hands of world-famous persons there are pointed out certain lines, which are characteristic of those qualities and talents that have been the mainspring of the achievements, fame or fate of these celebrities.

The older method of the science of reading the hand is commonly known as palmistry. Its more recent name is chirology, which is divided into two branches: first, chirognomy, and second, chiromancy.

Chirognomy is the branch which describes an individual's nature from the general form of the hand. It has been my experience that it is almost impossible to define character specifically or to delineate an individual's nature by the type of the hand alone, for exterior formation gives itself only to mere superficial observation. Generally, we divide the hands into seven main types, but there are certain aspects to consider first. The formation and physiological condition of the palm reveal the physical attributes of the possessor's character. For example: if the palm is thin, skinny and narrow, it undoubtedly will indicate timidity and the absence of depth of character and energy. On the other hand, if the palm is in perfect proportion to the fingers, thumb and rest of the body and is firm without being hard, it indicates an evenly balanced mind, which is appreciative, intelligent and capable of directing and controlling elementary instincts. In order to be perfect, the palm must be absolutely normally and naturally proportioned to the rest of the hand.

Many differences exist among hands. Two hands may look the same outwardly, but one may be so firm as to be hard while the other is soft, almost flabby. Such a cursory analysis indicates the possessor of the firm palm to be an active person; the soft-handed person to be quiet, reserved, imaginative, poetic and inclining towards an easy, pleasurable life. Thus, an artist with hard hands will paint things real and actual rather than the images of fancy portrayed by a soft-handed artist. Hard hands generally are more capable of true love, though not being very demonstrative about it, while soft hands denote more tenderness and affection than true love. It is an interesting fact to call to the reader's attention that, as we grow older, our hands become firmer, even to hardness. As the mind matures, so do the hands.

We become philosophic and less credulous, more logical and less romantic.

The seven types of hands are:
1. The elementary hand.
2. The conical, or artistic hand.
3. The spatulate, or active hand.
4. The square, or useful hand.
5. The knotty, or philosophic hand.
6. The pointed, or psychic hand.
7. The mixed hand.

The elementary type (plate 1) belongs to the lowest type of mentality and is largely a result of an uncultivated mind. It has a coarse, thick palm and the fingers and thumb are clumsy. Flexibility and grace are absent. This is the hand of coarse labor and unskilled avocations. The palm is longer in proportion to the whole hand; the fingers and fingernails are short. Very few lines show in this type of hand. Persons with the elementary type of hands have comparatively little mental capacity. They are phlegmatic and emotionless; their aspirations are limited. They eat, drink, sleep and die. Pure examples of such hands are rarely found among civilized nations, but are more often found among the primitive races and inhabitants of extremely cold climates.

The conical, or artistic type (plate 2), with slightly tapering palm and fingers slightly pointed at the tip and full at the base, is associated with an impulsive, impatient nature. The possessor of this type of hand is quick to grasp ideas, with intuitive judgment. Usually quick-tempered, such a person recovers just as quickly from fits of temper. He or she is known as "good company," but is apt to be changeable in friendship and affection, to be easily offended and to carry likes and dislikes to extremes. This type is easily influenced by others and, though generous and sympathetic, is often selfish concerning personal comfort. The artistic influence is induced more by color, music, eloquence, joy and sorrow than by genuine artistic feeling, for this is an emotional type, responding quickly to sympathetic influences.

Action, restlessness, energy and enthusiasm typify the spatulate, or active hand (plate 3), and the harder and firmer the hand, the more these characteristics are pronounced. Broadness either at the wrist or at the base of the fingers, and broad, flat fingertips identify this type as spatulate. Explorers, inventors, discoverers, engineers—persons with an intense love of action and independence—possess the spatulate hand, which characterizes its bearer as self-assertive, with marked individuality, advanced and liberal views, persistency and outspokenness. We find this type of hand to be characteristic of nearly all great men in the world of physical hardihood, active enterprise and applied science, who are brave, industrious and capable of surmounting obstacles. However, the spatulate type is apt to be strict, tyrannical and always ready to fight for his or her rights.

The square, or useful hand (plate 4) is typical of the born skeptic, who believes only what he or she sees and understands, and to whom practicality is preferable to the beautiful. This type of hand, whose palm is squared at the wrist and at the base of the fingers, and whose fingertips and nails show a decided squareness, is characteristic of natural reasoners with little originality, imagination or versatility.

YOUR FATE IS IN YOUR HAND

They are punctual, methodical, precise and orderly; as such, they lean decidedly towards material and practical things and usually achieve success. Being more influenced by custom and habit than any other type, they are great respecters of law and order but, though not quarrelsome, they are determined in opposition. Bearers of this type of hand are sincere, true friends; they keep promises and are honest in business.

Independence, indifference to material things and continual desire to find the true meaning of life are the essential characteristics of those who possess the knotty, or philosophic hand (plate 5), which is easily identified by its length, its bony fingers, well-developed joints and long nails. Such persons are great lovers of the pure sciences—moral, physical or experimental—and acquire their convictions only through careful analysis, being extremely meditative. An inborn sense of justice makes them just and tolerant in all forms of thought. They are fearless advocates of social and religious freedom, but recognize both sides of every question. Clarity and regularity of style mark their writings; moderation and near-asceticism, their pleasures. This type of hand is entirely free from superstitiousness.

In the long, narrow psychic, or pointed hand (plate 6), with its slender, tapering fingers and long, almond-shaped nails, we find a fragile beauty indicative of lack of energy and strength and a purely visionary, idealistic nature. Instinctive sympathy goes out to persons possessing this type of hand, for they characterize their owners as supersensitive and, as such, inclined to feel their position in life so acutely that they often consider themselves useless to the point of melancholia and morbidity. They are ruled by heart and soul, love the beautiful in every form, are confiding and instinctively trustful of those kind to them. Logic, practicality, order and discipline are beyond their reach. To many of such persons we owe the most beautiful and inspired poetry. Others make good mediums, being highly intuitive and sensitive to feelings, instincts and impressions. Refinement in manner and mildness in temper are characteristics of such persons, as is an attraction to magic and the mysterious. Their trustfulness makes persons of this type easily imposed upon, while their supersenitiveness makes them bitterly resentful of deception.

The mixed hand (plate 7) is so called because it cannot be classed with any of the aforementioned types. It is the most difficult of all to describe for the reason that its fingers belong to different types: one pointed, one square, one spatulate, etc. For the same reason, it identifies its owner as a "Jack of all trades but master of none." This is the hand of ideas, adaptability and general changeability of purpose. One possessing it finds almost any kind of work suitable and easy for him or her, but, because such a person also is changeable and unstable, he or she rarely achieves any marked success. This type of hand denotes great versatility which enables its bearer to meet all situations easily, because such a person is adaptable to circumstances and is not as acutely sensitive as others to the ups and downs of fortune. Enthusiasm over new ideas accompanied by restlessness characterizes this type with a lack of "stick-to-itiveness." Inventive inclinations are indicated.

CHAPTER II

The Thumb, Fingers and Nails

Considering all parts of the human hand, we find the thumb the most important, because it is a definite indication of the two greatest controlling factors of the human system: Will and Reason.

The thumb is divided into three sections: the first, or nail phalanx, which manifests will power; the second phalanx, indicative of reasoning power; and the third, or root phalanx, which is the barometer of passion. Great strength of will and purpose, strong character and constancy in friendship are evidenced by a long, well-developed nail phalanx. When this turns backwards, it characterizes its possessor as generous, possibly to the point of extravagance. As the second phalanx is in proportion to the first, reason controls the will; but, when there is lack of proportion between the two— when the thumb is unequally developed, with the nail phalanx exceptionally long and the second very short— will is the governing power. Conversely, when the second phalanx is longer and more developed than the first, the possessor has high reasoning powers but not sufficient strength of will or determination to carry out his or her ideas. A long third phalanx denotes control of passion; a short, thick one, a sensual nature. A long third phalanx in a comparatively short thumb is indicative of an individual who is prey to his or her more passionate and sensual nature.

The thumb is typed in three distinct classes (plate 8):

the clubbed, the supple-jointed, and the firm-jointed. The club-like thickness of the first class identifies an individual as belonging to the lowest type of humanity, so far as will is concerned. Because it manifests brutality, lack of control and liability to extreme violence in fits of temper, this type of thumb is often found in the hands of murderers, or those who commit crimes, not premeditated, but in fits of ungovernable passion or rage.

A flexible nature, adaptable, very broad-minded, unconventional and amenable, finds expression in the second type, or supple-jointed thumb, which indicates generosity of thought and money, an inclination to impulsiveness, sociability, and companionability. As a matter of fact, the latter tendency is a weakness to be guarded against, for, being charming companions, such persons give in easily to the wishes of others. Persons with this type of thumb readily enter into conversation with strangers and often make their greatest friends while traveling. The majority of them also like to take "the easiest way," but this characteristic is largely modified by the position of the Line of Head, which indicates developed will power. A supple second, or middle joint, which relates to the individual's reasoning powers, shows one to be adaptable to all circumstances.

Possessors of the third type, the firm-jointed thumb, which is the outward manifestation of a resisting nature, are cautious, and obstinate, seldom make friends easily and have a strong will and stubborn determination, which give them strength of character. Theirs is a keen sense of justice, though they are inclined to rule by might, and they have practical ideas of making the most out of life.

Fingers are essential indications of individual talents and capabilities. When straight, well-developed and in proportion to the rest of the hand, with their bases nearly level, they show qualities that make for success. Long fingers indicate love of detail, fastidiousness and quickness in noticing small attentions. Short fingers signify a quick, impulsive nature, more or less unconventional, outspoken, apt to jump at conclusions too hastily and disliking bother with little things. Extremely supple fingers that bend back easily denote a clever, rather inquisitive nature, full of life and charming in company. He or she, whose fingers are thick and puffy at the base, is fond of luxuries in eating, drinking and good living, with his own comfort always his first consideration. When naturally crooked, distorted fingers are found on a good hand—and this is rarely so—they signify an irritable person; but, when found on a bad hand, they indicate a crooked, evil and warped nature.

The index, or first finger, is called the finger of Jupiter. When it is straight and long, it is significant of strength of character and desire for power and command of others. Too long, this finger denotes a domineering and tyrannical person. When it is short, it reveals lack of ambition and dislike of responsibility. A crooked Jupiter finger signifies lack of honor.

Seriousness, love of solitude and reserve mark the possessor of a long second, or middle finger, which is called the finger of Saturn. When it is short, it signifies a frivolous nature with a general lack of seriousness.

The finger of Apollo, the third finger, is indicative of artistic tastes and desire for celebrity and fame, when it is long; but, when extremely long, it shows an inclination toward notoriety, love of money and gambling, and risk in speculation. A short finger of Apollo is a sign of dislike of all the things indicated by the long type.

A straight and long finger of Mercury, by which the fourth, or little finger is known, signifies mental capacity for making use of opportunities and talents, and brilliant power of expression, especially in speech. When this finger is short, it is a converse sign, denoting lack of tact and difficulty in expression. A crooked finger of Mercury, accompanying an irregular Line of Head, is an evil sign of twisted mentality. Good business ability and management of affairs is indicated by a square Mercury finger.

All of the fingers should be long in proportion to the palm to indicate good intelligence and mental powers. A wide space between the thumb and index finger denotes independence of will and fearlessness. Between the first and second fingers, a wide space shows independence of thought. When the second and third fingers are widely spaced, it is indicative of independence of circumstances, while a wide space between the third and little fingers denotes independence of action.

Fingernails are reliable guides to many diseases, for they have long been recognized by many medical men as capable of giving clues, especially to diseases of the heart, lungs, nerves and spine. Nails are reckoned under four separate classifications: long, short, broad, and narrow, each with its definite indications. Long nails signify a constitution that is not so strong as that of medium-sized nails. Long nails very wide at the top and of bluish tinge denote poor blood circulation. Persons with long nails are more likely to suffer from chest and lung troubles. Large moons manifest good blood circulation. Short nails show an inclination towards weak heart action, particularly when the moons are very small and hardly noticeable. When short nails are very flat and sunken into the skin at the base, they indicate a tendency to nerve disorders. Nails that are very long, narrow and curved are manifestations of spinal trouble and lack of energy. Thin nails denote very delicate health, when they are small. Short, red nails reveal a passionate, irritable disposition, while filbert-shaped nails signify a nature not easily roused to anger but, when once displeased, a nature that does not forget easily.

In disposition, persons with long nails are calmer, gentler in temper, and less critical than those with short nails. They are idealistic and artistic, with, as a rule, a fondness for beautiful things and the fine arts. They are apt to be visionary and to shrink from facing real facts, especially if those facts are unpleasant. On the contrary, short-nailed persons are extremely critical even of themselves, and, with clear reasoning powers and keen judgment, they like to analyze everything with which they come in contact. They have a keen sense of humor and are quite skeptical of all that they do not understand.

Needless to say, the habit of biting one's fingernails is an indication of a nervous temperament.

CHAPTER III

The General Principles of Chiromancy

Before coming to the most interesting and somewhat intricate part of chirology—that of chiromancy—let me impress upon the reader my sincere intention to make this book an up-to-date and, to the best of my ability, reliable guide in all matters connected with this science. From the very beginning, I have endeavored to clear this subject of all its inaccurate, doubtful, and so-called occult aspects, and to confine myself principally to information from authoritative sources, and that gathered from my own practical experience all over the world.

The science of hand analysis follows the same law of nature, which created in the human hand the remarkable phenomenon of the formation of rich patterns, each of which is so unique that there never have been two alike. Indeed, just as there are no two identical fingerprints, no two hands or natures are alike. But here I notice a peculiar phenomenon. While the rich patterns of the hand and fingers never change—and thus serve as the best medium for identification of the individual—the lines of the hands do change to some extent under the influence of mental and physical changes. While the lines retain the original patterns, they become indicators of development occurring in the course of life which relate to character, health, talents, inclinations and even events.

If you will compare your hands and their lines to those

represented by the charts presented in this book, you may detect, perhaps, in yourself certain dormant talents and qualities of which you have not been aware, but which, through the medium of this science, you will be able to cultivate. In so doing, you will find a natural way of expression or vocational adjustment. It is my belief that the most important factor in life is the discovery of one's aptitudes and talents, so that they may be developed to the fullest extent. It is equally important that one should know his or her limitations and shortcomings, so that they may be overcome. Therefore, I wish to emphasize that you can find the answer to most of your problems only in self-study and self-analysis. Asking another person's advice or guidance in any problem concerning yourself is like asking him whether or not he likes corned beef and cabbage. For no matter who is your advisor, you will find out merely what that advisor likes or dislikes, which may not apply at all to you. So why not study your own likes and dislikes? Also, I cannot over-emphasize the importance of the extreme care with which parents should choose vocations for their children. Mothers and fathers certainly should consider, in the greatest measure, the child's likes and dislikes.

In regard to foretelling the future, I am aware, of course, of the fact that most people are interested in hand-reading from this particular angle. So I take this opportunity to state my most candid opinion on this matter. The relation of shape and lines of hands to the shaping of the individual's life has been a matter of conjecture since the earliest civilization. The knowledge of the permanent formation of rich patterns in the hands and fingers, upon which the modern system of personal identification has been built, was known thousands of years ago. The Chinese and the old Hindu civilizations practiced hand-reading fifty centuries ago. We also find traces of its practice in ancient Egypt and Palestine. The real basis of the present-day science, however, was handed down to us by the ancient Hellenic civilization, for it was in Greece that hand-reading grew and flourished as a definite science. It found favor with and was practiced not only by the masses but also by men whose names forever remain immortal in the firmament of knowledge—Aristotle, Archimedes, Albertus Magnus, and many other celebrated thinkers and scientists way down into the Middle Ages. It is interesting to note that one of the first books ever printed, right after the invention of the printing machine by Gutenberg, was a book on palmistry by Aristotle published in 1475. A copy of it is to be found in the New York Public Library.

There never has been any branch of human knowledge that has not been degraded, at one time or another, by being exploited by charlatans. Even up to the present day unscrupulous "quacks" are using the name of medical science for duping the ignorant and credulous with cure-alls. Therefore it is no wonder that hand-reading, or what is more commonly known as palmistry, with its inherent mystery, has been considered, as in the Middle Ages, as an occult science, or has been used by gypsies, fortune-tellers and fakers as a means of exploitation of the superstitious.

The pretense of being able to foretell the future has never failed to lure the gullible public. The fact that hand-reading has been misused in this way does not discredit a scientific study of the subject. Here I wish to state most emphatically that no one can, with certainty, predict events of the future! To me, the analysis of the hand and its relation to obtaining physical and mental conditions has no connection whatever with fortune-telling. As the science of medicine is limited to a prognosis and diagnosis in forecasting the cause of a certain disease, so the analysis of the hand is limited to the recording of certain signs indicating mental and physical conditions, and drawing from their total, conclusions as to the probable developments and changes.

Many people wrongly imagine that the lines on the palm are caused by hard work, while the reverse of the case is true. The hand of a ditch-digger or any other manual worker, as a rule, has few lines except those principal ones, which very few hands are without, namely, the Lines of Life, Head, Heart, Destiny, etc. On the contrary, a rich society woman, who may care little to exert herself to pick up a handkerchief, will frequently be found to have her palms covered with a network of fine lines.

Work and all kinds of active games or sport will steady the nerves, distract the thoughts from self and, instead of making lines, will smooth out those that have appeared previously and prevent the formation of others. For it is feelings and emotions affecting the brain that act upon the brain and leave the record of what the individual has gone through, in reality or in imagination. Events and experiences in one's life, even though tragic, may leave no impression, if the person is of a phlegmatic nature or is one who forgets easily.

The theory of chirology is based upon the fact that the

human hand, being connected directly with the brain through the blood stream and supersensitive nerves, reflects on the palm the thoughts and impressions, conscious or subconscious, that agitate the brain, or experiences that have left an impression on the mind. Hence, I want to impress upon the reader the fact that no lines, however big or small, are "mere creases"! The lines are not stationary, they grow, alter and disappear. A many-lined hand denotes nervous temperament and inclination to worry. Hands of women, generally, display more lines than hands of men, because their nerves are weaker and their feelings more acute. The hand of a person who is not susceptible to any depth of feeling, shows very few lines. It is also true that no line, whatever it may indicate, is unalterably final. Any disaster or fatality indicated on that particular line may be just a sign-post or warning of danger, which one may escape through knowledge of this science.

As you read further in this book, you will see hands which I have identified of famous personalities in all walks of life. No doubt you will be curious as to how I arrived at these conclusions. In my travels around the world as a newspaperman, I interviewed thousands of world-famous personalities, outstanding in every line of endeavor. What most amazed me was finding, in the hands of these celebrities, certain lines definitely indicating their individual talents. For example, I found in the hands of brilliant musicians a similar combination of lines indicating their musical talents. This particular combination is not found in the hands of those who are not gifted musically. So it was in every other vocation. Certain lines indicated certain talents and qualities. After I had analyzed many thousands of these hands, it was a comparatively simple matter to catalogue the meaning of the various lines and combinations of lines.

I am sure that my presentation of the following brief sketches, together with the charts of the hands, will provide the reader with a fascinating pastime as well as a beneficial study. Compare your hands with those given here and see if you can find similar lines to show you either conscious or subconscious qualities and inclinations.

CHAPTER IV

The Principal Lines of the Hand

Seven principal lines predominate in the human hand. The Line of Life, or longevity, embraces the Mount of Venus. The Line of Head, or mentality, crosses the center of the palm. The Line of Heart, which is significant of the emotional side of the individual's nature, runs parallel to the Line of Head at the base of the fingers. In the center of the palm, the Line of Fate, or destiny, runs from the wrist to the Mount of Saturn. The Line of Apollo, or success, rises from the center of the palm and ascends to the Mount of Sun, or Apollo. The Line of Health, or Hepatica, runs down through the palm from the Mount of Mercury. On the side of the palm and at the base of the Mount of Mercury lies the Line of Marriage. (See Plate 9.)

Among the lesser lines, the Line of Mars, or inner life line, rises on the Mount of Mars within the Line of Life. The Girdle of Venus is found above the Line of Heart encircling the Mounts of Saturn and Apollo. Like a semicircle, the Line of Intuition runs from the Mount of Mercury to Luna. The Bracelets are found at the wrists. The Ring of Saturn encircles the Mount of Saturn, while the Ring of Solomon is found under the finger of Jupiter.

Before discussing in detail these various lines, let me say something briefly about the general aspects. Lines should be clear and well marked, neither broad nor pale, and should be free from breaks, crosses, islands and other ominous signs. Lines reddish in color denote an active, energetic and hopeful nature, while very pale lines conversely indicate delicate health and lack of energy. Very dark lines manifest a melancholy temperament inclined to morbidity, revengefulness and relentlessness. Lines may appear, diminish or fade, but there is always a reason for such an occurrence. It may be a warning of approaching danger or oncoming success. It may point out to the individual, tendencies to be cultivated or repressed, but it rests with the individual's will to overcome or control such tendencies. Danger or disaster indicated in the lines of the hand can be avoided. A network of tiny lines running in all directions is indicative of mental worry and a highly nervous temperament. A chained formation of any line denotes weakness of some sort, while a break in the line manifests failure of some sort connected with that particular line. Branches rising from a line accentuate its strength; those descending, its weakness.

I want also to consider both the right and the left hand briefly, for usually there is a marked difference between the two hands. The left hand is indicative of hereditary traits, the ambition, desires, and fears of the individual. Too, it is the hand of characteristics, talents and possibilities. In the right hand, we find how far these latter have been cultivated and developed, for this is the hand registering favorable growth of character or retrogression, development of hereditary tendencies or their arrested state, and improvement in health or the reverse. In the right hand, also, lie the signs by which future possibilities are judged.

Incidentally, left-handedness is nothing more than a manifestation that the left-handed individual's entire nervous system is focused on the left side, with the left eye dominating vision. Left-handed children should not be forced by parents to change to their right hands, for such an attempt might cause behavior disorders, such as irritability, seclusiveness, lying, or even theft. Left-handedness is no mark of inferiority.

Now we come to a detailed consideration of the lines of the hand. The Line of Life, or longevity, lying directly over the large blood vessel, which is connected with the heart, stomach, and other vital organs, enables us to presuppose the length of life from natural causes. In the left hand, it shows the inherited constitution of the individual; in the right hand, the illnesses gone through and those that may occur. This line should be long, clearly marked and devoid of any breaks to indicate a long life, vitality and a strong constitution. Also, since this line represents the vital organs, it necessarily signifies, if the line is well marked, that the stomach and digestion are in good condition. Both hands should be compared very carefully before a warning of approaching illness or liability to any disease is given. A break in this line denotes illness or debility of health, being accentuated if found in both hands. However, care taken during the period of life where the break occurs may mend the line or cause a double line to appear as the danger passes. A short Line of Life does not necessarily indicate an early death but it is a sign that the possessor exercise caution at the age where the line ends. If vitality and resistance are built up again at such a time, the line will grow longer than it was originally. The most significant foreshadowing of death is the termination of all principal lines at the same date. When the life line ends in a star or cross, it is an omen of sudden death or accident. When the life line sends a branch out toward the Mount of Luna, it indicates death in a foreign land after long residence there. When the line is composed of little sections, or is linked like a chain, it is a certain sign of poor health, weak stomach and lack of vitality. However, ascending branches on the life line denote a life of great energy at the age when such branches make their appearance. When the life line begins high up on the palm at the base of the Mount of Jupiter, it signifies that the individual has good self-control and that his life will be ruled by his ambitious nature; rising lower down on the palm, it indicates less control of temper.

Very broad lines signify a predominance of muscular strength over will power, while clear, deep, thin lines show that the will is superior.

The Line of Head, which relates to the mentality and to the temperament in its relation to talent and imagination, can normally rise from three different points in the palm: from outside the Line of Life near the center of the Mount of Jupiter; from inside the Line of Life on the Mount of Mars; and joined to the Line of Life. The commencement and termination of this line should be carefully noted, for it shows the direction toward which the mentality is inclined to develop. For instance, if the head line lies in the same position in both hands, it shows that the individual has been permitted to follow his natural inclination; that is, he was given free rein in the development of his natural mental inclination. On the other hand, if the Line of Head slopes downward in the left hand but is straight in the right hand, it is evident that the individual has undergone some strain in early years, has not been able to follow his natural inclinations and has been forced by circumstances into a profession different from that he desired originally. You can understand, then, how important it is to make your study of both hands a careful one.

The rise of the head line outside of the life line at a not very wide distance is a powerful sign indicative of individual energy, talent, mental daring, boundless ambition and clear reasoning powers. It is the sign of the natural born leader, quick to grasp ideas and to think, to whom a definite purpose in life is extremely important, for, without such, this individual may drift aimlessly. The same rising point of this line widely spaced from the life line denotes a nature with very little caution and sensitiveness, which will go to extremes, desires notoriety, lacks continuity of purpose and is changeable and excitable. The same type of head line, not far from the life line and terminating under negative Mount of Mars, is indicative of the self-appointed leader of public movements, who will sacrifice everything for what he believes is his public duty.

When the Line of Head starts inside the life line on the Mount of Mars, it is the sign of a highly nervous, supersensitive, timid nature with very little self-control or check on temper. Such a person is easily offended. This type of line is found mostly in the palms of persons inclined to intemperance of every description.

The Line of Head joined to the life line is indicative of a very sensitive, self-conscious nature, which lacks self-confidence to some extent. It often signifies that its possessor undervalues his talents and abilities. As this particular type of line bends downward in the palm, sensitiveness is accentuated; it is found in the hand of the person with a sensitive, artistic temperament. When it runs straight across the hand, it indicates a sensitive nature but one with self-control. This type of line curving gradually down toward the Mount of Luna denotes a vivid imagination controlled by the individual and used only as he wishes, but, as this line bends down abruptly and ends with a curve under the base of the Mount of Luna, it signifies an extremely morbid imagination and so sensitive a nature that the individual is inclined to lead a life of solitude or to end it by suicide.

The straighter the Line of Head, the more determined the individual to carry out his ideas. When the line is forked, with the two lines of the fork of equal length, it indicates a dual mentality, practical on one side and imaginative on the other. The person with this sign should follow his first impulse always rather than lose valuable time in indecisiveness. A straight, clear and even Line of Head indicates a practical common-sense nature with good business qualities. When it is extremely long and straight and running directly to the side of the palm, it evidences high intellectual powers and a somewhat selfish nature. As the head line curves upward slightly, it means that its bearer will develop an intensity of purpose and achieve success in business or in any profession involving financial transactions. When the normal Line of Head turns at the end or sends a branch to any particular mount, it shares the qualities of that mount. Such a branch running toward the Mount of Luna denotes vivid imagination and inclination to mysticism; toward the Mount of Jupiter, great ambition and pride; toward the Mount of Saturn, seriousness and depth of thought; toward the Mount of Apollo, prominence and success; and toward the Mount of Mercury, science and business.

If the Line of Head is very high on the palm and placed close to the heart line, it means that the head completely rules the heart. Conversely, if the heart line is nearer to the place where the Line of Head normally lies, the heart rules the head. When the head line is broken in two in both hands, it signifies some fatal accident or a great shock to the head. When this line runs through a square, it denotes preservation from accident or violence to the head through the individual's own presence of mind. If both the Line of Head and the Line of Heart are merged into one line, which runs clear across the palm from one side to the other, it is not a very happy mark, though it indicates tremendous intensity of character and great concentrative powers. The person with this mark can't seem to make friends, often feels very lonely and isolated, and can be successful only when working alone. A double Line of Head, though seldom found, indicates a dual nature and great brain power. It denotes extreme sensitiveness and gentleness on one side, self-confidence and craftiness on the other; but it also signifies versatility, fluency of language and a strange personal magnetism.

The Line of Heart, indicator of the emotional side of the nature, normally rises under the Mount of Mercury and runs across the upper part of the palm to the base of the Mount of Jupiter. It should be clear, deep and well-colored.

As this line terminates in different points, it denotes various characteristics. Ending at the outside of the Mount of Jupiter, it shows the bearer to be one who usually goes to extremes, a blind enthusiast in love who is carried away by his feelings beyond all reason and who, consequently, suffers greatly because he wastes his affection often on those unworthy of it. If the heart line ends in the center of the Mount of Jupiter, it denotes a very ambitious nature, strong and reliable in affection and possessed of a high type of love. When it ends between the first and second fingers, it indicates a calm, quiet but deeper nature in matters of love. Terminating on the Mount of Saturn, the heart line signifies a very passionate, sensual and often very selfish nature. A broad and chained line ending on this mount denotes utter contempt for the opposite sex.

When the Line of Heart is very long, extending from side to side, it is a manifestation of an extremely jealous disposition; if it is very red in color at the same time, there is indication of great violence of passion. A broad and pale heart line denotes an indifferent nature, blasé in love. When this line lies low in the palm close to the head line, the heart will always interfere with reasoning. Breaks in the heart line signify disappointments in love. Branches reaching out from the Line of Heart to other parts of the palm indicate good fortune and happiness in love, but, when the line is thin and bare, it denotes a cold, selfish heart. When bare and thin at the side of the hand, it denotes sterility. If the Lines of Heart and Head are very close to each other, they reveal a narrow-minded character engrossed in its own affairs. However, if the space between the two lines widens towards the end under the Mount of Mercury, the ideals and interests of the individual are capable of development.

Events of life, changes, successes or failures, barriers and obstacles, possibilities of the future and the ultimate result of one's career are read in the Line of Destiny. Although this line generally runs across the center of the palm between the wrist and the Mount of Saturn, there are many variations. If, in this normal course, this line sends out branches to any other Mount, it indicates that the individual's life will be greatly influenced by that particular mount. When such a line sends a branch to the Mount of Luna, especially in the hands of women, it denotes a wealthy marriage but also an ideal one. If an offshoot runs toward the Mount of Jupiter, it signifies unusual influence over others, responsibility and, generally, success; if towards the Mount of Apollo, success in riches and prominence in public life; if towards the Mount of Mercury, achievement in the field of science or commerce. When the Line of Destiny runs through the palm as a single line devoid of branches, it marks its bearer as a plaything of Fate, unable to control his own life and a puppet to the force of circumstances. It is not considered a happy mark, especially when such a line runs right on up the Mount of Saturn into the finger for it shows that everything its possessor undertakes will get out of his control.

However, the Line of Destiny may have its starting-point in many different places in the palm, each with its special significance. When it rises from the Bracelets and runs straight up the center of the hand to the Mount of Saturn, and, when, at the same time, the line of Apollo is well marked, it is a brilliant sign of unusual luck, success and good fortune. If this Line of Fate rises from the Line of Life, it indicates eventual success to be achieved by the individual only after early years of difficulty and obstacles. Surmounting of such impediments of early life to become a "self-made man" by his own effort is certain, if this line runs clear and strong where it leaves the life line. As the Line of Destiny rises from the Mount of Luna, it speaks for a very changeable fate, but an eventful one, largely dependent on the whims and good will of others—a mark often found in the palms of actors, writers, statesmen and public favorites.

A career to be handicapped by one's own folly or stupidity is indicated, when the Line of Destiny appears to be stopped by the head line. Foolishly placed affections will mark the career of the individual whose fate line seems to be stopped by the heart line; but, if the fate line joins the heart line and they ascend together the Mount of Jupiter, great happiness, realization of ambitions and luck and success in everything undertaken will be attained through love and affection.

Difficult early life is denoted by a fate line first appearing in the center of the palm; success late in life only through the effort of the individual's own brain, by a fate line starting from the Line of Head. A career of romance and passion is indicated, when this line sends branches out to the Mount of Venus and to the Mount of Luna. A break in the Line of Destiny usually omens a change in one's career, but, if the line is broken up considerably into little lines, it signifies a very unsettled life full of difficulties and trouble. The fate line ending abruptly with a cross augurs a life to terminate through some tragic fatality. The absence of any Line of

Destiny in a hand denotes a phlegmatic character leading a colorless and very ordinary life.

The Line of Apollo, or success, rising from the center of the palm and ascending to the Mount of Sun, or Apollo, increases the good fortune portended by a good Line of Destiny and is a certain sign of fame and success. A magnetic personality marks the possessor of this sign, who easily wins recognition, wealth and honors and who is endowed with a happy disposition. From the first appearance of this line in the hand (it may not occur until mid-life), the individual becomes brighter and more prosperous. If the line rises from the Line of Life, it promises success in artistic work, if from the fate line, ultimate success in a career adopted and brought about by the individual's own effort. Rising from the Mount of Luna, it promises in the hands of artists, actors and persons in the public eye, good luck and recognition. A Line of Apollo starting at the head line indicates great success through individual mental effort, being a brilliant sign in the hands of brain workers such as scientists, inventors, writers, etc. As it starts from the heart line, it presages a happy marriage late in life. Difficulties and notoriety are indicated by a cross on the Line of Apollo, but a star on this line is a most brilliant and fortunate sign for it is indicative of great wealth, honors and realization of one's ambitions and desires. When a hand has no Line of Apollo, its possessor will find great difficulty in gaining recognition in this life, no matter how brilliant, clever or talented.

Examination of thousands of hands has assured me of the reliability of the Line of Health, or Hepatica, as a more accurate indication of health than any other mark in the palm.

Total absence of this line is the best sign of all, for it indicates a very robust, healthy constitution. However, its presence serves as a warning to the individual. Usually it starts at the Mount of Mercury and runs down the hand. The straighter it lies down the hand, the better, for that indicates a constitution which offers more resistance to disease than a line crossing the palm, though it does not signify a particularly robust physique.

Indications of the other principal lines of the hand, especially of the life and head lines, are important to consider in conjunction with the health line. If the life line seems very weak and chained, the Line of Health naturally increases the danger of illness; if the head line appears broken or chained, the health line foreshadows some brain disturbance. When the health line crosses the hand and touches the Line of Life, it indicates the presence of some germ in the system, which is undermining it. If the health line runs down the palm and into the life line, it presages the advent of an illness, which, at the time when it touches the life line, will reach its final crisis. A Line of Health rising from the heart line and running through the life line denotes weakness or disease of the heart. A very red health line, broken into small parts, indicates a tendency toward fever. Bad digestion and liver trouble are indicated by a twisted, irregular health line. A deeply marked health line running only between the Lines of Heart and Head is a symptom of impending brain fever. If the Line of Health is marked as deeply as the life line, their union at any point augurs almost certain death to the individual, despite the length of the Line of Life.

The Marriage Line, or Lines, will be found at the side of the hand on or at the base of the Mount of Mercury. This line lying close to the Line of Heart indicates early marriage; when lying midway between the heart line and the base of the finger of Mercury, marriage at about twenty-five or twenty-seven years of age. However, only the deep, clearly formed lines relate to marriage; the short, lighter ones are significant of deep affections only. The possessor of a marriage line that turns upward most likely will never marry. A marriage line dividing into a fork towards the end indicates separation and divorce, if it turns further down into the hand. A very distinct Line of Marriage with little lines curving downwards denotes delicate health of one's mate and the probability that the person, whose hand bears this mark, will outlive his or her mate. A broken marriage line, linked like a chain, is a warning that its bearer should never marry, for such a marriage would be unhappy. However, a Line of Marriage running into the hand and ascending towards the Line of Apollo augurs a very rich and happy marriage. Also one of the most certain indications of a happy marriage is an influence line running from the Mount of Luna to join the Line of Destiny, especially when combined with one very distinct, outstanding line on the side of the palm under the finger of Mercury.

Tiny lines ascending from the Line of Marriage on the side of the hand are indications of children and, as a rule, are seen more in the hands of women than in those of men. Broad, deep lines signify male children; fine, narrow lines, females. The number of these small lines, counting from the outside of the hand toward the palm, indicates the number of children the bearer will have. Very straight lines indicate strong, healthy children, while very faint, uneven lines are indicative of very delicate children. One of these lines appearing stronger and superior to the others is an indication that one child will be more distinguished by its gifts and talents than the rest. An exceptionally flat Mount of Venus, combined with an arch-like rise of the first Bracelet up towards the palm, is an almost certain sign of sterility.

Among the lesser lines of the hand, the Girdle of Venus, at the base of the fingers above the Line of Heart, rises in a broken, or unbroken, semi-circle between the first and second fingers, encircling the Mounts of Saturn and Apollo, and ends between the third and fourth fingers. It is indicative of a highly strung, supersensitive, nervous nature which is touchy and easily offended. The bearer of such a mark is very changeable in moods, going from one extreme to another. If the Girdle of Venus continues across the hand to touch the Line of Marriage, it signifies that the individual's peculiar temperament will make the happiness of his or her marriage difficult to preserve.

The Line of Intuition (The Via Lasciva) is a strange and unusual mark, which is found mostly in the hands of psychic, philosophic or artistic types. Such a line, which is sometimes called the second Line of Head, appears as a semi-circle running either from the Mount of Mercury to the Mount of Luna; from the Mount of Luna to the wrist; or from the Mount of Luna to the Mount of Venus. In the first-mentioned position, it reaveals a high strung, sensitive nature with an acute sense of intuition, which manifests itself in feelings of presentiment and in strange, vivid dreams that very often come true. Women bear this mark more than men, but, whenever it is found, it denotes remarkable power and a faculty of which the possessor may not even be aware. It induces an inspired state in even the most uneducated bearers of the mark, endowing them with an extraordinarily accurate knowledge which they cannot explain. Even more remarkable is the fact that the use of alcohol, drugs or any stimulant destroys such strange powers.

A Line of Intuition running from the Mount of Luna to the wrist indicates an over-sensual imagination and sensual dreams and desires, with a tendency towards a craving for drugs and excessive use of alcoholic drinks. It also marks its possessor as having no control over himself in other directions. In conjunction with a broken Line of Head that descends towards the Mount of Luna, this line is a warning that extravagance, or even insanity, will eventually destroy the individual's career and life. In the third position, the Line of Intuition is indicative of great passion and sensuality. As this particular formation runs from the Mount of Luna to the Mount of Venus and cuts through the Line of Life, it augurs death for the individual due more to excessive high living than from ill health.

The Bracelets, the three lines encircling the wrist, are supposed to indicate the length of life, health and happiness, but modern chirologists do not give them much consideration. However, one indication is given by the first Bracelet, when it appears broken in half and turns up towards the palm, for it combines with a low Mount of Venus to denote almost certain sterility.

The Ring of Saturn, which encircles the Mount of Saturn, is a rare sign, fortunately, because it is not a good sign. It denotes a very changeable temperament, full of ideas and plans but without the will and persistence to carry them out. The person whose hand is marked with this sign, never succeeds, for he or she lacks the ability to concentrate on any one thing. Such an individual also is gloomy and inclines to morbidity with a feeling of isolation from the rest of the world.

Under the finger of Jupiter, the Ring of Solomon is a very strange sign denoting love of the occult or mysterious. Arching from between the first and second fingers to the outside of the hand, it indicates the ability of its possessor to master that inclination.

The Mystic Cross is another strange sign, which lies in the center of the palm between the Lines of Heart and Head to indicate a superstitious nature inclined towards mysticism and occultism. The shorter the head line, the more superstitious the individual. When the Mystic Cross appears high on the hand, it denotes superstition regarding one's own life.

One of the most fortunate and brilliant marks to possess in the hand is the Star. When it lies on the Mount of Jupiter, it presages great power and honors; on the Mount of Apollo, great wealth and public prominence; on the Mount of Mercury, remarkable eloquence and success in business or science; on the Mount of Mars under Jupiter, distinction in a military career; on Mars under Mercury, distinction achieved through the individual's mental courage and brilliancy; on the the Mount of Venus, success and magnetic power over the opposite sex; on the Mount of Luna, fame and glory resultant from the individual's imaginative faculties. The only unfavorable location for the Star to be found is on the Mount of Saturn. Though it denotes distinction, it is an ominous sign for its possessor's life will end in some frightful disaster, a fate which will bring him fame.

The Cross, with the exception of location on the Mount of Jupiter, where it indicates an ambitious nature and the promise of at least one great love, is an unfavorable sign. On the Mount of Apollo, it is an unhappy sign of disappointed ambitions and desires; on the Mount of Mercury, of a dishonest nature; on the Mount of Luna, of too vivid an imagination, and self-deception; on the Mount of Venus, of a very unhappy love affair. The Cross on the Mount of Mars, under Jupiter, signifies danger of violence, and possibly death, from quarrels; on the same mount, under Mercury, it indicates opposition of powerful enemies. Great danger from accidents is omened by a cross on the Mount of Saturn, when it touches the Line of Fate. A cross on the Line of Head augurs an injury to the head; on the Line of Heart, death of a loved one.

Another very unfavorable mark is the Island. Appearing on any one of the mounts, this sign greatly weakens the attributes of that mount. On the Line of Life, an island indicates a delicate condition, especially of the vital organs, and illness. Islands in a continuous chain on the Line of Head denote hereditary weakness of the brain; a single island on the head line, under the Mount of Saturn, shows a tendency toward nervous headaches. Under the Mount of Apollo, an island indicates over-strained eyes, but, when such a mark occurs on the heart line under that mount, it denotes a tendency to weakness of the heart. An island on the Line of Destiny signifies losses and worry about the future; on the Line of Apollo, loss of position because of scandal; and on the Line of Health, serious illness.

A Circle on the Mount of Apollo is a favorable sign, but, situated on any other mount, this mark threatens danger of drowning.

The Square is an excellent mark for the hand for it is indicative of preservation and protection, and, as such, denotes escape from dangers and preservation from losses in one's career and life.

Grilles are usually found on the mounts, and are signs of difficulties attendant on the portions of the hand in which found. On the Mount of Jupiter, a Grille indicates inordinate pride and a desire to dominate; on the Mount of Saturn, despondency and a melancholy nature; on the Mount of Apollo, vanity and notoriety; on the Mount of Mercury, a changeable, unstable nature; and so on, each mount's quality being affected.

The Great Triangle, formed by the Lines of Life, Head and Health enclosing the center of the palm, denotes a generous nature, liberality of thought and broadmindedness, particularly when the triangle is broad. The absence of the health line and substitution of the Line of Apollo for the base of the triangle is one of the greatest signs of power and success. If, however, the triangle is bounded by three small, uneven lines, it is a sign of meanness and a timid, cowardly spirit.

The Lines of Head and Heart form the Quadrangle, which should be straight, even in shape, and not crossed by many lines. So marked, this sign indicates great intellectual power, a well-balanced mind, loyalty and sincerity in friendship or affection. If, however, the Quadrangle is very narrow, it signifies narrow mindedness, pettiness of thought and bigotry in respect to religion and morals. On the contrary, an excessively wide Quadrangle in its entire length is a sign of an unconventional, reckless and imprudent nature. Smooth and free from little lines, a Quadrangle indicates a very placid disposition, but, when crossed by too many tiny lines and crosses, it denotes a restless, irritable temperament.

Correct calculation of time and age can be made by dividing the Lines of Life, Head, and Destiny, into periods of seven. This is a most natural division, since important changes in the human constitution take place every seven years. To make such a chart, draw an imaginary line on the Line of Life, reckoning downward, and beginning under the Mount of Jupiter on the Line of Head from the place where it leaves the Line of Life toward the side of the hand, and the Line of Destiny from the Bracelets up, running toward the Mount of Saturn.

LOOK AT YOUR HAND

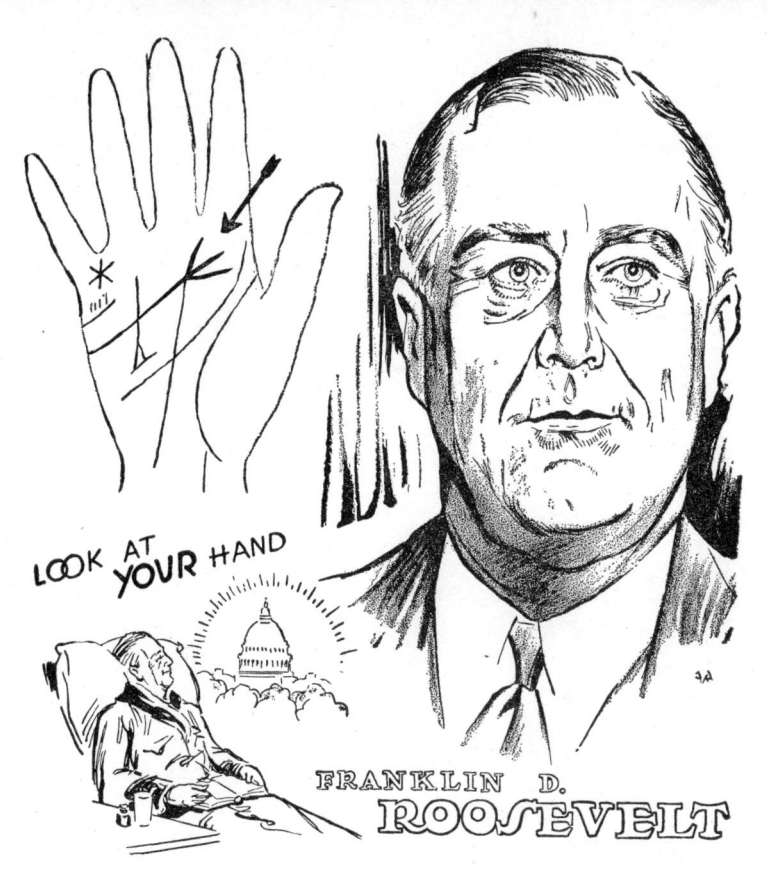

FRANKLIN D. ROOSEVELT

IS YOUR predominant characteristic magnificent courage, as it is Franklin D. Roosevelt's? Look at the small lines extending from the line of heart in his hand, pictured above. If those lines are duplicated in your own hand, you have with the President, a character to whose supreme courage no obstacle is insurmountable. They are called THE LINES OF UNDAUNTED COURAGE.

Franklin D. Roosevelt's ascendency to leadership of these United States bears witness to his indomitable spirit. His rapid rise in law and statesmanship is well known. Infantile paralysis, which wracked his vigorous body in 1921 and bound him to practical immobility for months, failed to quench the courage that was later to write him into United States and world history as an invincible Spartan. As Governor of New York State his record stands approved—approved by all but political influences to which he refused to cater. The people whom he represents are his "friends." He has taken the "forgotten man" under his understanding wing. He moved into the White House on promises which he made good. And he has been justly acclaimed the greatest President of the United States since his illustrious relative, Theodore Roosevelt. No petty politics swerved him in his fight to restore prosperity. From his great courage he gave new courage to the "man on the street"; he assumed in his rights as Executive-in-Chief the powers he deemed mandatory in a time of extreme emergency; and his invincible will restored confidence to his people and jobs to unemployed.

BENITO MUSSOLINI

LOOK AT YOUR HAND

HOW does your hand compare with that of the iron man of Italy? Notice the squares surrounding the breaks in the principal lines in his hand, pictured above. They denote escape and preservation from great dangers and injuries, and if you find them in your own hand the same beneficent fate will be yours. They are called THE SQUARES OF PRESERVATION.

The star seen underneath Mussolini's first finger indicates great power and brilliant success as a leader of men. "Il Duce" has risen to outstanding prominence in world history as Fascist leader and Premier of Italy, whose forty millions he has molded into strong unity. As a disciplinarian, he has astonished the world. It was a strange twist of destiny that catapulted this former school teacher, who could not tolerate the arbitrary discipline of the classroom, to international acclaim as a severe taskmaster. The destiny that protects this Iron Man of Italy has evidenced itself many times in his miraculous escape from maniacal assassins, as it did during the World War from which he emerged with the scars of forty-two wounds. From a radical, he changed to an ardent patriot and nationalist. What he has done so far for Italy is only a part of his destined accomplishment, for these same lines indicate a long and fruitful life.

Page 48

The PRINCE of WALES

LOOK AT YOUR HAND

ARE you destined to become noted for your sportsmanship, like the Prince of Wales? Look at the base of your first finger. If you see a triangle there like the one in the Prince's hand, pictured above, you are a born sportsman. It is called THE TRIANGLE OF SUPERIOR SPORTSMANSHIP.

The Prince of Wales, heir to the throne of England and probably one of the most popular and famous men alive, has greatly endeared himself to the public by the way he forces himself to the front in the world of sport. Hunting, tennis, golf and his habit of riding his own horses in competition with crack jockeys over stiff steeplechase courses thrilled even the non-sporting public, for the danger in steeplechasing is great even to the brilliant horseman. Another interesting line in his hand is his line of marriage, found underneath the fourth finger pointing upward, which is an indication that he may never marry, in spite of the fact that his picture probably draws more soulful glances from the debutantes of two continents than that of any other man.

Page 49

LOOK AT YOUR HAND

ADOLF HITLER

HAVE the fates drawn a veil across your future, so that no man may read it? Look at the line which ascends Adolf Hitler's palm without branches, running like a lonely path up into the base of the second finger. If you have this line, like Hitler, your destiny, whether splendid or sad, will be clouded and uncertain to the end. It is called THE LINE OF UNCERTAIN FATE.

The cross seen at the termination of Hitler's life line foreshadows a violent end. Adolf Hitler, leader of the German Brown Shirts, whose phenomenal rise to power has been as spectacular as the menace of his doctrines to the peace of the present-day world, possesses that peculiar type of personality which remains as intangible as most of his theories. This writer interviewed Hitler and analyzed his hand in August, 1930, under very dramatic circumstances. Subsequently, he wrote in an article his belief in Hitler's imminent rise to power, which will be followed by his violent end and chaos in Germany. It is the conviction of this writer, now more than ever, that this fiery Nazi leader cannot escape the impending doom which the lines in his hand so eloquently reveal.

Page 50

LOOK AT **YOUR** HAND

J. RAMSAY MacDONALD

WILL your future be as brilliant as that of the Prime Minister of England? Look for a line beginning underneath the first finger, crossing the palm curving slightly downward in the center and ending at the side of the hand. It denotes high idealism, logical reasoning and the strong conviction that right takes precedence over might. It is called THE LINE OF BRILLIANT STATESMANSHIP.

This beloved Scot, Ramsay MacDonald, who rose from humble, obscure beginnings to be Prime Minister of England, is a modern parallel of Abraham Lincoln. Raised in the sturdy simplicity of the Scottish coast, he turned to politics at an early age. At 20 he removed to London as a business office clerk to devote his spare time to reading and study. In 1888 he became secretary to a member of Parliament; then a free-lance journalist active in the labor movement. Twice defeated as Labor candidate for Parliament, he was finally elected to the House of Commons in 1906. In the next eight years he rose to leadership of his party. His rise was rapid after the World War. Made Prime Minister in 1924, he is now serving in that capacity for his third term. As a leader and personality he is a strange paradox, being perhaps one of the best-loved and, at the same time, most-hated man in Great Britain. In his convictions he is loyal to no party but to the nation as a whole. He has made sacrifices for his ideal—the welfare of that nation which gives him its love and trust.

Page 51

POPE PIUS XI.

How does your hand compare with that of His Holiness Pope Pius XI? If at the top of your palm between the first and second fingers you see a star, you, too, have qualities of spiritual leadership. This star is very often seen on the hands of high church dignitaries. It is known as THE STAR OF SPIRITUAL LEADERSHIP.

The 261st successor to the throne of St. Peter was born in Italy in 1857 of peasant stock. His inclination for the Church showed itself at an early age. At 10 he became a student in the Seminary of St. Peter the Martyr at Milan and later, was admitted to Lombard College in Rome. He took his degrees of cannon law, theology and philosophy at the Gregorian University and was ordained priest in 1879. From 1882 to 1917 he was chaplain of a monastic institution in Milan, later becoming prefect of the Vatican library. It was as apostolic nuncio to Poland that he revealed the courage, even temper, firmness and diplomacy that were later to make him Pope. The writer had the honor of meeting him in 1920 during the Polish-Russian War, when the Soviet Army was at the gates of Warsaw, and of reading his hand signs which gave promise of the great honors awaiting him. In 1921 he was made Cardinal, and, in 1922, he was chosen by the conclave as sovereign Pontiff. His efforts to establish harmony between the Church and the State, his public appearance and broadcasting to the world at large have made him a great contributor to democracy.

LOOK AT YOUR HAND

GRETA GARBO

ARE you destined to go through life wrapped in glamour, a fascinating enigma to all who know you? If you see a line encircling the base of the index finger as in the illustration of the Great Garbo's hand, you may be sure that you have a natural gift or talent for emotional expression, which may be in either drama or music. It is called THE LINE OF EMOTIONAL MOODS.

Greta Garbo, whose names has become synonymous with glamour in acting, and who is possibly the most highly paid of living women, was born in Stockholm on September 18, 1905. of parents in comparatively poor circumstances. She worked as soap girl in a Swedish barber shop and as salesgirl in a dressmaker's establishment before going on the stage. Brought to America by Moritz Stiller who early recognized her talent, her brilliant portrayals won her almost immediate recognition as a star. Her personal fascination and exotic appeal were enhanced from the beginning by her air of mysterious aloofness and reluctance to talk about herself, a trait scarcely typical of Hollywood, yet almost single-handed she has altered the technique and style of the motion picture. and is perhaps the greatest screen actress of our generation. Her unusual talents can be easily seen in the lines of her hands.

Page 53

LOOK AT YOUR HAND

JOHN BARRYMORE

DOES your hand reveal that you have great possibilities as an actor, possibly unknown to you? Look for a line ascending from the lower side of the palm toward the base of the third finger, plainly apparent in Barrymore's hand, pictured above. This line signifies extraordinary ability and recognition in the world of make-believe. It is called THE LINE OF BRILLIANT DRAMATIC EXPRESSION.

John Barrymore was born in 1882, in Philadelphia, the youngest child of that distinguished American theatrical family affectionately known as "The Royal Family." As a boy he wished to become an artist, and even studied art in London and New York. When he was 21, however, he made his stage debut and thereafter continued in that field. His really great triumphs came when he played in Galsworthy's "Justice," in "Peter Ibbetson," in Tolstoy's "Redemption" and finally in "Hamlet," which he played 101 times in New York City alone, breaking the record of Edwin Booth. He even dared the Shakespearean "hoodoo" of London with his production, to score in the most notable success a Shakespearean play has had there since 1600. When he returned from England he declared his intention of entering the movies and has, since that time, confined himself entirely to a screen career, in which he rules as a star of first magnitude. He is now married to Dolores Costello, herself a screen star and daughter of a great actor, Maurice Costello.

Page 54

LOOK AT YOUR HAND

AMELIA EARHART

DOES your hand hold the sign of great courage? Look for small lines, running from what is known as the line of the head into the base of the first finger. These lines are clearly seen in the illustration of Amelia Earhart's hand, and they signify dauntless courage and great mental daring. They are called THE LINES OF DAUNTLESS COURAGE.

Amelia Earhart Putnam, the only woman ever to fly over the Atlantic twice, first became actively interested in aviation after the war. In 1920 she established the woman's record for altitude. She was also the first woman to whom an international pilot's license was issued. After her first flight across the Atlantic with Wilmer Stultz and Lou Gordon, she became aviation editor of a magazine. Her solo flight across the United States was the first to be made by a woman, and the following year she took part in the women's derby from Los Angeles to Cleveland. Her ambition to make a solo flight over the Atlantic, was realized when she made her spectacular flight from St. John's, N. F., to Londonderry, Ireland.

Page 55

LOOK AT YOUR HAND

PAUL von HINDENBURG

WILL you live a long and glorious life, like President von Hindenburg of Germany? If your life line—the line beginning under the first finger, running down the palm and encircling the heel of the thumb—is extremely long, as in Von Hindenburg's hand, pictured above, you may be sure that you will have a long and active life. It is called THE LINE OF LONGEVITY.

In the career of this beloved militarist lies proof of that destiny Today at 86 he is still active as President of the German Republic Born in 1847 of a long line of soldiers and statesmen, he had his first active military service in the Austro-Prussian War of 1866 as a second lieutenant. Conscientiously he climbed laboriously through routine garrison life and academic studies toward the apex of the military hierarchy. Discipline and duty were always his guiding factors. In 1909 he retired, as yet unknown to public life. The World War brought him from retirement to take command of Germany's Eastern forces. He smashed the Russian onslaught and became Germany's most popular idol overnight. In 1925, at President Ebert's death, he was persuaded to run for office by monarchists who thought his election would eventuate the return of the Kaiser. Von Hindenburg disappointed them in his rigid adherence to the constitution, though since Hitler's advent he has allowed his royalist sympathies to become more apparent.

LOOK AT YOUR HAND

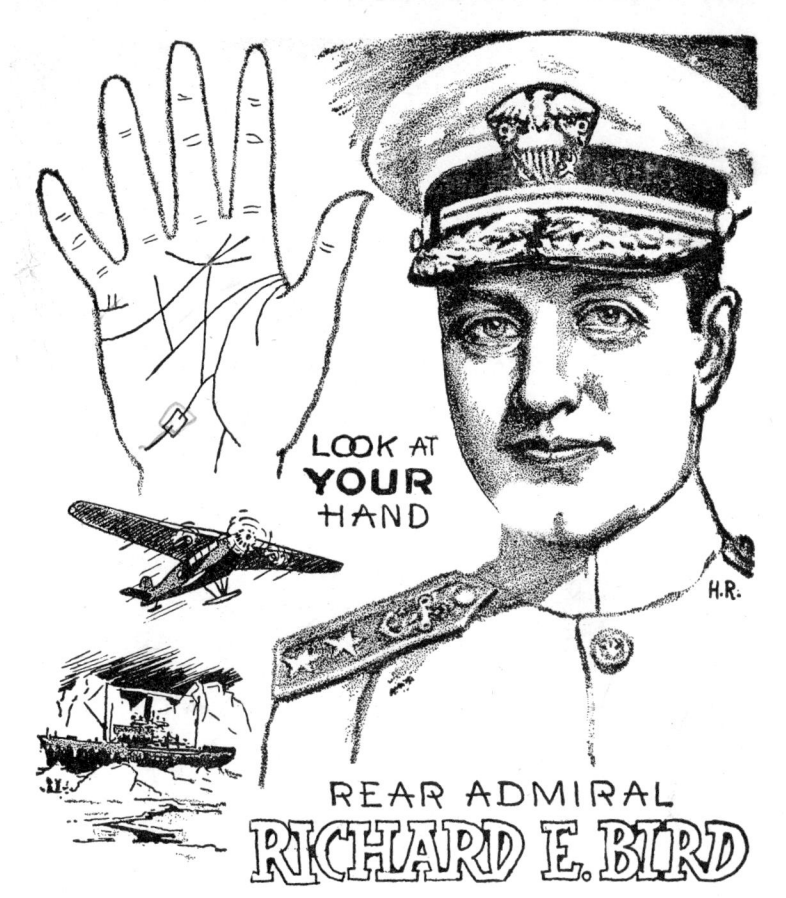

REAR ADMIRAL RICHARD E. BIRD

IS YOUR life, like Admiral Byrd's, destined to be filled with thrilling adventure? Look for a line at the bottom of your palm running toward the side of your hand, like that clearly defined in Byrd's hand, pictured above. This line denotes a life replete with exploration and daring. It is called THE LINE OF TRAVEL AND ADVENTURE

The square seen on a break in this line in Admiral Byrd's hand denotes grave danger, but, being a mark of preservation and glory, it denotes safe passage to world acclaim. This venturesome Virginian who sailed alone around the world at 14, has lived his destiny with rare courage and self-reliance. Lured by the Arctic, his explorations carried him to great historical achievements. Graduated by the United States Naval Academy in 1921, he eagerly pursued the study of aeronautics, the progress of aviation having instilled in him a determination to explore by air. In 1925, in the naval air service, he was designated flight commander of the MacMillan expedition, which flew 3000 miles into the Arctic wastes. A year later, with the late Floyd Bennett at the controls, he made his courageous flight from Spitzbergen to the North Pole. For this, President Coolidge awarded him the National Geographic Society's Hubbard gold medal "For Valor and Exploration." After a trans-Atlantic flight from New York to France, he next turned his eyes toward the Antarctic. There he flew over the South Pole and established "Little America."

Page 57

LOOK AT **YOUR** HAND

PROF. EINSTEIN

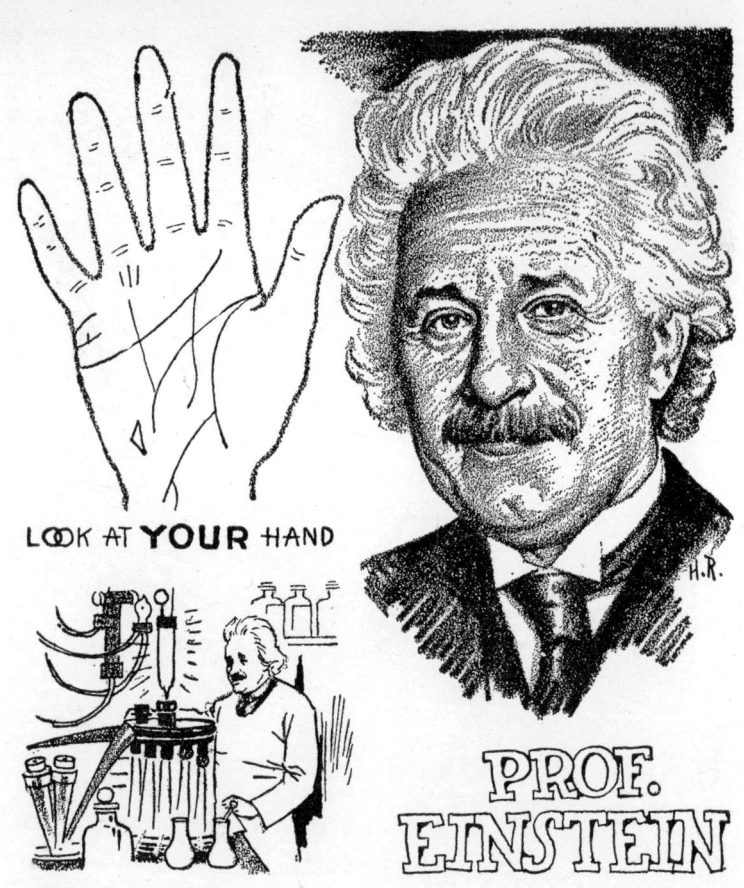

DOES your hand show the signs of a brilliant scientific mind? If you have three short lines at the top of your palm, midway between the third and fourth fingers, you have a keen, analytical mind and a brilliant ability for scientific research. These lines are clearly shown in the illustration of Prof. Einstein's hand. They are called THE LINES OF SCIENTIFIC GENIUS.

Prof. Albert Einstein, who has devoted his life to developing a scientific theory which only a dozen men could understand, and who succeeded in captivating the imagination of the world with one word —"relativity"—was born of Jewish parents in Ulm, Germany. Although he reached a high place among the world of scientists at the age of 26, when he published his theory of relativity concerning gravitation and light rays, it was not until the final proof of his findings that he became world famous and was awarded the Nobel Prize for Physics. Aside from his scientific genius, his traits are candor, wit, simplicity and an open mind for every human accomplishment. Despite his own contention that he is merely a physicist, he is looked upon as a philosopher an artist, a humanitarian who takes an eager interest in aiding mankind

MARLENE DIETRICH

(LOOK AT **YOUR** HAND)

DOES your hand show the distinguishing characteristic which has lifted Marlene Dietrich to fame? Look for two lines at the base of your first finger, extending from what is known as the line of heart. These lines reflect a magnetic personality and eloquent eyes, both present in the glamorous actress and clearly indicated in her hand, illustrated above. These lines are called THE LINES OF EYE MAGNETISM.

Marlene Dietrich displayed great talent from her early childhood. It was her early ambition to become a concert violinist, but an injury to her left wrist halted this career and she turned to the stage. She had been playing small parts for some time when Joseph Von Sternberg, who brought her to America, was in Berlin looking for a leading lady to play opposite Emil Jannings. Since her advent in America she has taken her place in the rank of the foremost stars. She has developed her own unique style of acting and has built up a vast following in her own right. It is not so well known that she is also a singer of great charm and ability. One of her main attractions seems to lie in her eyes, for if ever an actress was able to convince an audience that the essence of beauty is a gaze profound and haunting. complex and provocative. it is this young German film star.

Page 59

LOOK AT **YOUR** HAND

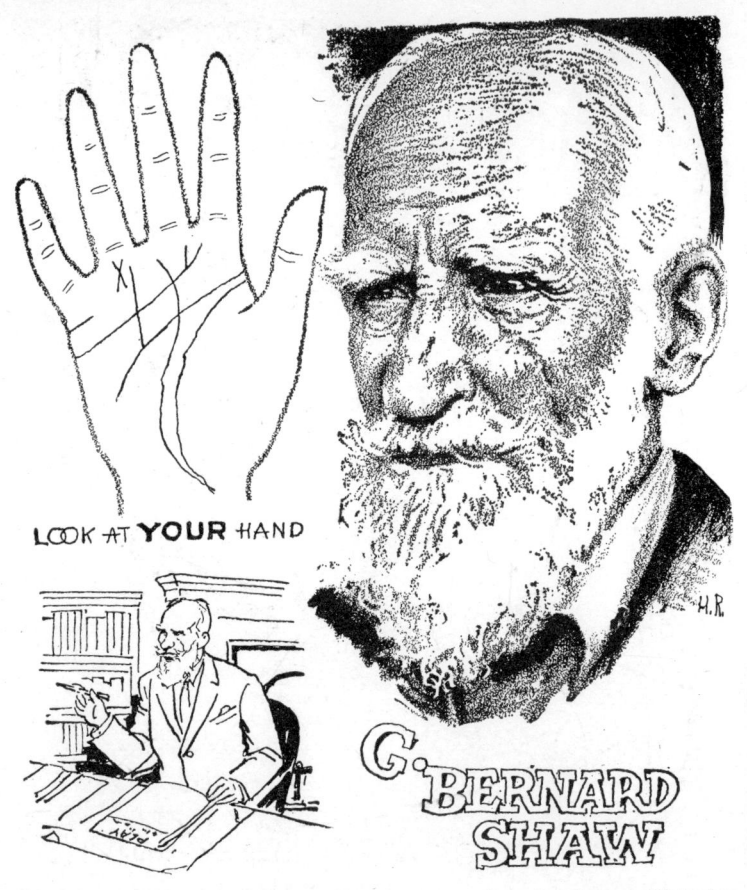

G. BERNARD SHAW

ARE you destined to become famous for your brilliant wit, like George Bernard Shaw? Look for a line rising from the center of the palm upward to the base of the third finger. It is clearly shown in the illustration of Shaw's hand, and signifies a career that should reach great fame and renown purely by the efforts and qualities of one's own mind. It is known as THE LINE OF INTELLECT AND WIT.

The shape of George Bernard Shaw's hand, known as the "philosophic," denotes great literary talent, an aptitude for wit and satire, yet a somewhat lonely and ascetic disposition. Shaw has, in spite of his comic mask, been as effective and sincere a teacher as any man alive today. Born in Dublin, Ireland, he went to London at the age of 20 and threw himself headlong into radical movements, joining in the general onslaught on Victorian morality and becoming a convert to vegetarianism and Karl Marx. In his first nine years in London he earned precisely nine pounds by his writing, of which five was for writing a patent medicine advertisement. Three years later he was writing for a morning paper, an evening paper and a weekly review on music and the theatre, and writing plays in his leisure time. Ten years later he published his first group of plays. In 1903 he produced "Man and Superman," which proved an immense success. He is primarily a sociologist, writing plays instead of textbooks, and using the theatre as his lecture hall, coaxing the public to hear his message by wrapping that message in spontaneous wit.

LOOK AT YOUR HAND

JOHN D. ROCKEFELLER

How does your hand compare with that of John D. Rockefeller? Look at your so-called "life" line. If it begins under the first finger and runs down the palm, encircling the heel of the thumb, you may be sure that you will have a very long and active life. It is called THE LINE OF LONGEVITY

The shape of Mr. Rockefeller's hand, shown in the illustration, particularly the squareness of the palm, portrays a man full of untiring energy, a methodical and enormous worker, stubborn and determined in whatever he goes after, winning by the sheer force of his indomitable will.

John Davison Rockefeller, the world's first billionaire, was born in a little frame dwelling in Richford, New York, on July 8, 1839 When he was 14 years old, young Rockefeller got his first job as a clerk at a salary of $50 a month. When he was nearing 21 he asked for $800 a year, and upon being refused, resigned and went into business for himself. He became acquainted with Samuel Andrews, an engineer, who had invented a process for refining oil. Rockefeller took him into partnership, out of which was to grow the Standard Oil Company. At one time the capitalization of the companies he controlled was placed at $5,000,000,000 and his personal fortune at $1,000,000,000. With the money he amassed by careful and astute business methods—never by speculation—he began to lay plans for philanthropies on a hitherto unparalleled scale. At present, at the age of 94, he is still hale and hearty.

LOOK AT YOUR HAND

COL. CHAS. A. LINDBERGH

DOES your hand show the sign of fame which presaged Lindy's glory? Look for a line running from the center of your palm toward the base of your third finger. If you see a star at the end of the line, as in the illustration of Lindbergh's hand, you have a personality which, under proper circumstances, is able to gain and hold immortal fame and glory. It is called THE STAR OF IMMORTAL GLORY.

Colonel Charles Augustus Lindbergh, who became the Nation's idol and the aviation hero of the entire world by his solo flight to Paris, attended the University of Wisconsin for two years, then decided to become an aviator. After a course at a flying school he bought an old army plane with which he did barnstorming stunts all over the country. Later he attended the army flying school at Brooksfield, Tex., and was commissioned captain of the reserve forces. Later flying a dangerous route as a night air-mail pilot, he conceived the idea of the non-stop flight to Paris. On the morning of May 20, 1927 with virtually no publicity, he headed his plane toward Paris and fame. After his return from Paris he made a national tour of the country, then flew to Mexico as the country's goodwill Ambassador. It was there that he first made the acquaintance of his wife, Anne Morrow Lindbergh, daughter of the late Dwight W. Morrow.

LOOK AT **YOUR** HAND

MARY PICKFORD

ARE you destined to become a public idol, like Mary Pickford?

Look for a line ascending from the base of the palm at the side of the hand toward the base of the first finger, like that clearly shown in the illustration of Mary Pickford's hand. This line denotes a personality which can win popularity and acclaim, and is particularly significant in the hands of actors, public speakers, artists and similar people. It is known as the line of public favoritism.

Mary Pickford, who with her golden curls and winsome smile became America's most popular and highly paid motion-picture actress, made her stage debut at the age of 5, when she played the part of a little boy. At 9 she was already a full-fledged star. Her first screen appearance was in a series of one-reel productions, for which she received a salary of $40 a week. Her rise in the film world was swift and sure, and when her contract expired in 1918 she refused to sign again, although she was receiving a mammoth salary, preferring to establish herself as an independent producer. Her splendid acting and clean, wholesome film stories did much to lift motion pictures to a high plane in the amusement world, and for years the picture public would not let "Our Mary" grow up. The golden curls and childish, appealing ways of "America's Sweetheart" still hold their appeal, and her popularity continues undiminished with a public which is notoriously fickle and unstable with its idols.

Page 63

BOBBY JONES

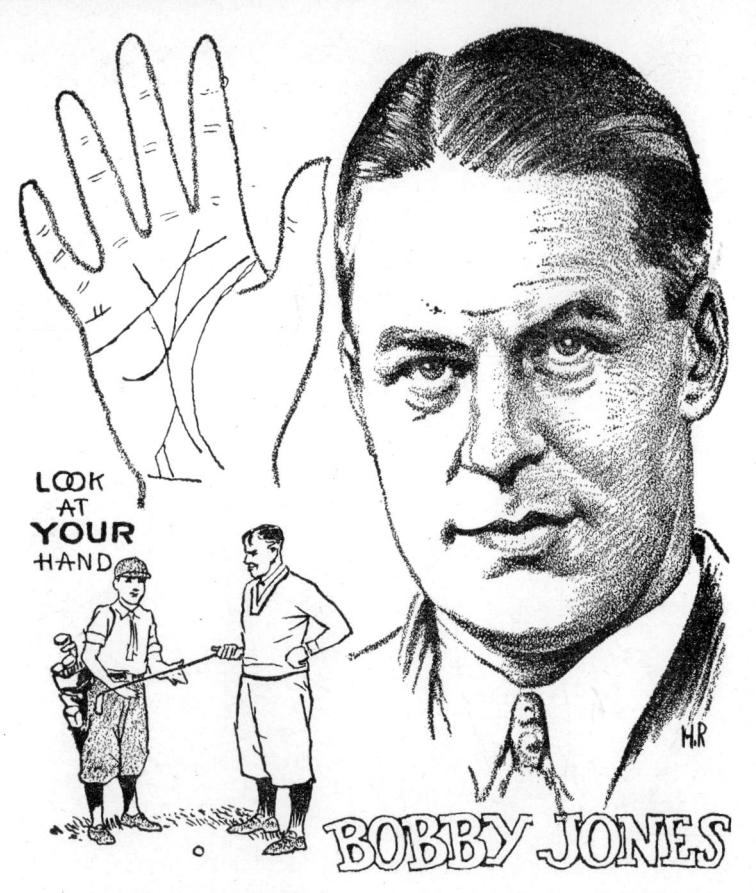

LOOK AT YOUR HAND

WILL perfect accord of mind and muscle win you fame as it has Bobby Jones? Look for a line extending in an upward curve from what is known as the line of head. The line of head begins under the first finger and runs straight across the palm, and the uptilt at the end denotes perfect concentration and unusual co-ordination of mind and muscle. This curve is plainly apparent in the illustration of Bobby Jones' hand. It is known as THE LINE OF MENTAL AND MUSCULAR CO-ORDINATION.

Robert Tyre Jones, Jr., undisputed king of all golfdom, was a frail and sickly child. When he was 5 years old an attending physician told his father to get the boy out in the open and keep him there. He was given a tiny set of golf clubs and taken to a golf course. By the time he was 8 he had developed such a fine swing and was getting such prodigious distance on his tee shots that he entered as a contender in the Georgia junior championship for boys ranging in age up to 18 years. He won this championship twice in succession. His enthusiasm, supported by inborn qualities of mental and muscular co-ordination, finally brought him both the United States and British open championships. He conquered all the golf worlds there were to conquer and announced his retirement from competitive golf after he had made the most brilliant record in the history of the game.

LOOK AT **YOUR** HAND

HENRY FORD

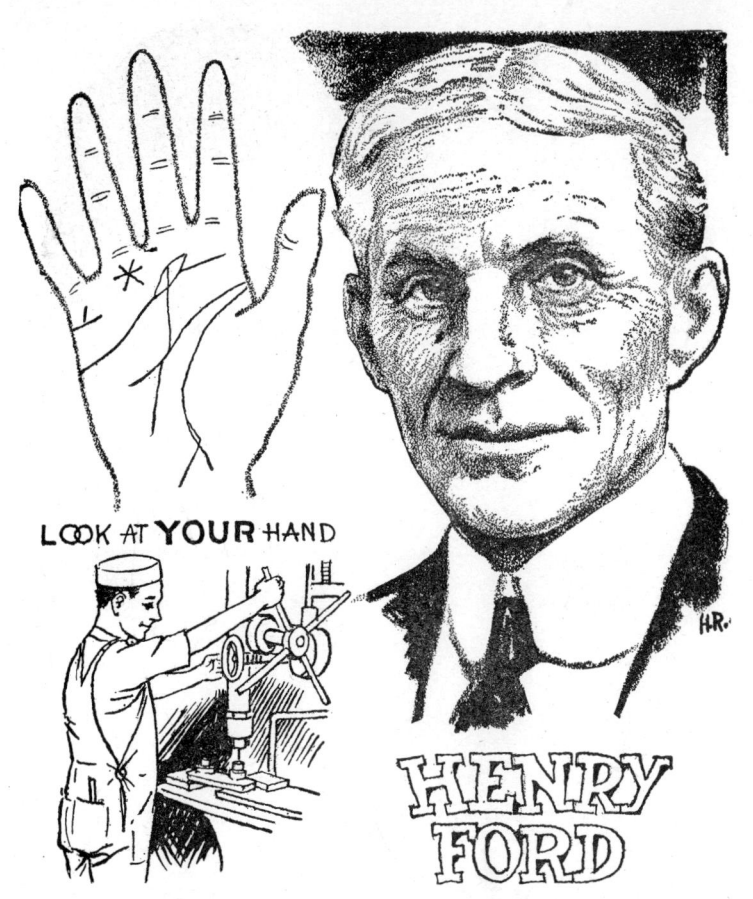

HAVE you in your hand the marks of mechanical genius which raised Henry Ford from a poor boy to the wealthiest man in America? Look for a semicircle underneath your middle finger, like the one shown in Henry Ford's hand. This is a very rare mark, signifying world-wide recognition and usually great riches as a result of superlative skill in mechanics. It is called THE SEMICIRCLE OF MECHANICAL GENIUS.

As a youth, Henry Ford knew all the hard work that is the lot of the average farm boy. As he grew older he began to wonder why the farm, as well as the factory, could not profit by the amazing development of the machine. From that pondering sprang the germ of an idea, and from the idea grew one of the greatest industries of the twentieth century. He built his first car in 1895. It had two cylinders, developed four-horse power, had a close resemblance to a buggy, and was regarded everywhere as a nuisance, with crowds flocking about it and holding up traffic. In 1903 he organized the Ford Motor Company, and the first year sold 1708 cars. Twenty-five years later the daily average was five times that of the entire production of the first year. In 1914 he created a sensation by establishing $5 as the minimum wage for an eight-hour day. By 1924 financial experts agreed that he was the world's richest individual.

Page 65

LOOK AT **YOUR** HAND

HELEN KELLER

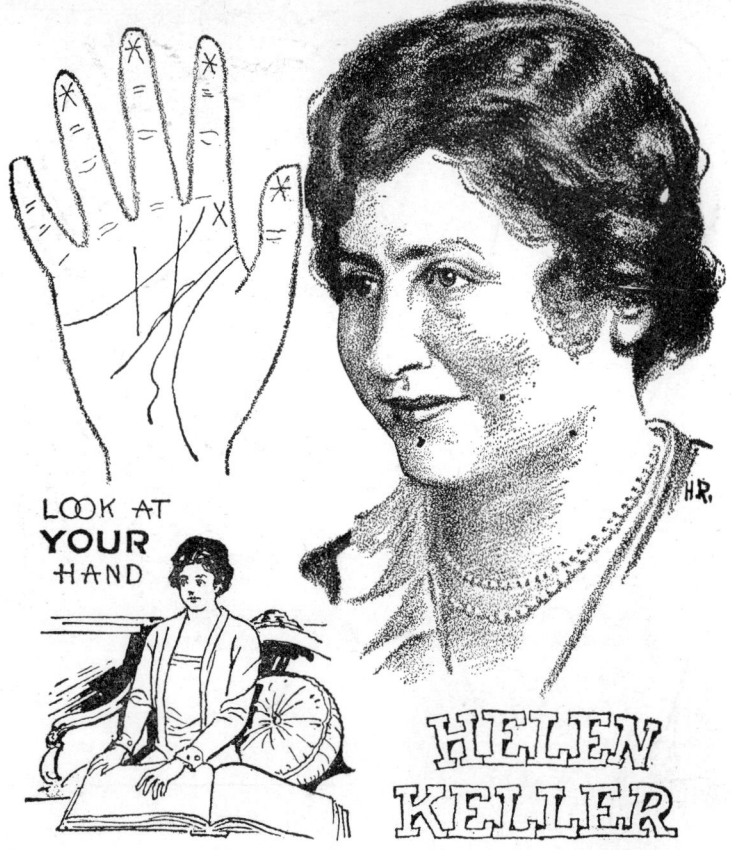

HOW does your hand compare with the remarkable hand of Helen Keller, the most famous deaf and blind person in the world? In the illustration of her hand you will see stars on four of her fingers. If you also have these stars, it means that, like her, you have such an acute sense of touch that it is possible actually to see, hear and talk through them. They are called THE STARS OF UNUSUAL FACULTIES.

Helen Keller was a bright, healthy baby, who had learned to walk and was learning to talk when, at the age of 19 months, she was taken seriously ill with brain fever. After the illness left her she was discovered to be totally and irrevocably blind, deaf and dumb. At the age of 7 she was taken in charge by Miss Ann Sullivan, who has never since left her. She taught the girl to make up for her lost senses through the use of her hands, and directed her intelligence to such good purpose that Miss Keller earned a bachelor of arts degree in a higher institution of learning. In the years following her graduation from college she wrote a number of books and traveled and lectured all over the world. Although her whole life has been a struggle, she is essentially gay, spirited and sturdy. She permits no one to pity her. Miss Keller has participated in every major movement for the uplift of the blind, and has herself been the subject of endless scientific experiment and philosophical speculation. Few persons have ever had to battle such handicaps as hers; few persons have ever achieved such a triumphant victory over them. She has become not only a symbol but an inspiration.

Page 66

LOOK AT **YOUR** HAND

JOSEPH STALIN

ARE you destined to become a leader of men, like Joseph Stalin, Dictator of Russia? Look for a star a short distance beneath your first finger, as in the illustration of Stalin's hand. If you find it, you have an iron will that employs every means to reach its goal. This star is known as the star of powerful leadership.

Soviet Russia's "man of steel" holds in his hands the destinies of her millions, for his colorful life has led him to the dictatorship of that vast nation. Born in 1879 of peasant stock, he launched upon a career in the church. Revolutionary doctrines, both Nationalist and Marxist, seeped into the confines of the seminary, and Stalin became a leader of the Marxist circle, for which he was expelled. From then on he has crowded into his life more fighting action than any other modern ruler. Under the Czarist regime, he was imprisoned six times, escaped five, and was jailed for seven years as a political revolutionist. Professional agitator for the Social Democrats, he organized strikes and demonstrations. It was while he was in jail in Baku in 1902 that he came in contact with the Bolshevist party, to which he became a strong supporter. Escaping from Siberian exile, he organized branches of that party in the support of Lenin and from then until 1917, when imperialism was overthrown, he was generally in the thick of violent revolutionary activities. But nothing was able to break his iron will and undaunted determination. Today he wields greater power than that of a czar.

GENERAL JOHN J. PERSHING

ARE you destined to win fame as a soldier, like General Pershing? A star at the base of the thumb, clearly seen in Pershing's hand, gives the clue. This sign indicates great distinction in military life. It is known as THE STAR OF MARTIAL GLORY.

General John J. ("Black Jack") Pershing has marched steadily upward through a military career with a strength and modesty that have endeared him not only to his commands, but to the world at large. Born in Missouri in 1860, he won an appointment to West Point to begin a military reputation which has made him one of the greatest of American heroes. In Indian warfare, in the Philippines, in Japan and in Mexico he distinguished himself. But it was the World War that gave him his greatest laurels as commander-in-chief of the American Expeditionary Forces in France. His mastery of that command is a matter of history. First, he held his ground successfully against the British and French, who wanted to send the newly arrived Americans into the front lines. Pershing held out for a distinct American unit, benefited by all possible training. Leaving France at the close of the war with the last departing division, he returned to America to succeed General March as Chief of Staff of the United States Army in 1921. He retired in 1924, but thereafter served as special official representative of the Government to Europe, to Peru and to South America on special occasions.

LOOK AT YOUR HAND

CLARENCE DARROW

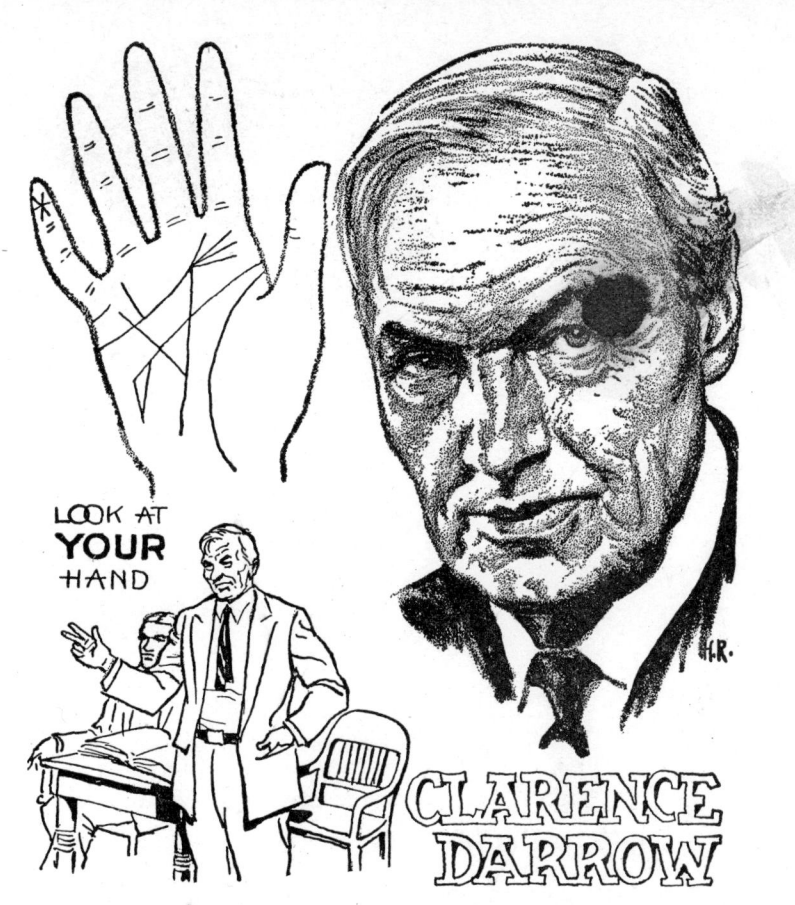

HAVE you, like Clarence Darrow, the gift of eloquence which sways men to do your will? Examine your fourth finger. If you find a star at the tip, you have the kind of power of speech whose logic and simplicity spellbinds listeners. It is called THE STAR OF ELOQUENCE.

Clarence Darrow, famous criminal lawyer — champion of the oppressed—is gifted with a greater persuasive eloquence than any living contemporary. Born the son of a clergyman in Ohio in 1857, he studied law and was admitted to the bar in 1878. He relinquished a profitable connection with the Chicago and Northwestern Railroad Company to defend Eugene V. Debs and others in the great railroad strike of 1893. From then on he has devoted his career primarily to the cause of human rights and lost causes, when he has felt justice threatened by the might of the majority. His sympathetic fight for labor is well known. His belief in the influence of heredity and environment is given as an explanation of his defense of criminals and his opposition to the "eye-for-an-eye" axiom. To this end he has often defended cases without fee. His eloquence is brilliant; his intellectual power dominating. He can pour oil on troubled waters as easily as he can annihilate an adversary with piercing satire.

Page 69

ALFONSO XIII

LOOK AT YOUR HAND

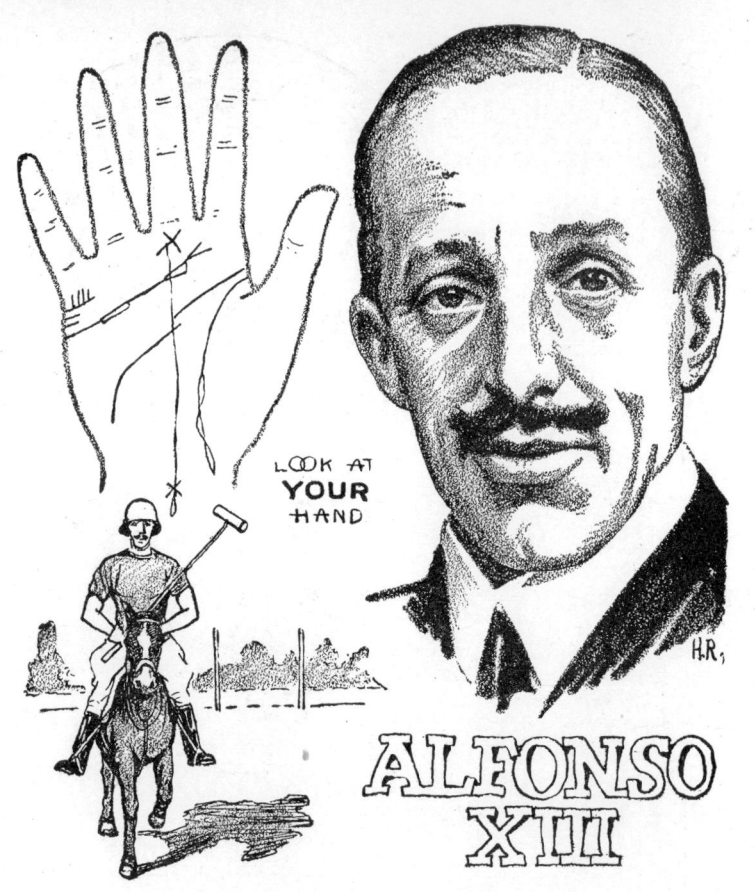

IS YOUR desiny hidden in the uncertainties of the future, as is ex-King Alfonso's, of Spain? If your fate line runs through the center of your hand without branches, running like a lonely path up and onto the base of the second finger, your life, like his, will probably be swayed by external circumstances. This line is known as THE LINE OF UNCERTAIN FATE.

This unhappy monarch's fate, which began when he was born six months after his father's death to become Alfonso XIII, King of Spain, he has accepted resignedly with a chivalrous fortitude that has marked his entire life. During his minority, when his mother, Queen Christina, ruled as regent, he was a target for assassins, as he was in later years. At 16 he ascended the throne to a disheartening career beset by revolutions and anarchists. But an indomitable courage and persistency held him to his "job as King" as he called his sovereignty. The revolt of 1931 forced his abdication, which he accepted fatalistically with the democratic sportsmanship for which the world knows him. Peacefully, he relinquished the royal heritage of his kingdom. Courageously, he wrote the historic finale to the romance of the House of Bourbon. And bravely, he lives in exile with his family.

Page 70

LOOK AT **YOUR** HAND

CHARLEY CHAPLIN

How does your hand compare with that of the inimitable Charlie Chaplin, beloved genius of the films? Look at your hand; have you a line starting at the bottom of your palm from the termination of the Line of Head, rising upward and terminating in a small triangle underneath the second finger? This line is clearly shown in the illustration of Chaplin's hand, and signifies a nature somewhat gloomy in its outlook, with a genius for portraying the droller side of life. It is called THE LINE OF COMIC TRAGEDY.

None who have chuckled at the whimsical comedy of Charlie Chaplin, master pantomimist, or have wiped away stray tears at his so-human pathos, could but hail him King Comedian of his day. The son of traveling players, Chaplin displayed his unusual talents at an early age. He first came to America from his native England in 1910. Starting as a vaudeville clown, the originality of his unique make-up made the early Chaplin a sensational success. In the later films, of which he is the author, however, he has raised the level of his early work to the unsurpassed heights of the sentimental-grotesque comedy in which his genius found its real expression. The touching character of the hopelessly incompetent, philosophic, lonesome vagabond **is** an unapproached dramatic creation, and bears out the truth of the line of comic tragedy marking Chaplin's palm.

Page 71

LOOK AT YOUR HAND

GEORGE ARLISS

ARE you destined to become a great actor? Look at the termination of your line of head: If you find a tripod there you may become as splendid in the theatre as George Arliss, whose hand, illustrated above, shows this mark clearly. As a rule this sign denotes great talent in the theatre. It is known as the tripod of brilliant acting ability.

George Arliss was born in London, the son of a printer and publisher. After graduating from school young Arliss spent a year working in his father's business and dabbling in amateur theatricals in the evenings. Finally he made up his mind to follow a theatrical career. During an engagement with Mrs. Patrick Campbell his popular appeal was established. In "Disraeli," "Alexander Hamilton" and "The Green Goddess," followed by John Galsworthy's "Old English," which proved tremendous successes, his sparkling portrayals created theatrical history. Then came the "talkies" and his portrayal of Disraeli in the motion picture of that title, which was awarded the Photoplay Gold Medal as being the outstanding motion picture for the year 1929. Mr. Arliss, never handsome, depending on features which are interesting and aristocratic but irregular, has gained the greater part of his success in character roles.

Page 72

LOOK AT YOUR HAND

IGNACE PADEREWSKI

ARE you destined to become as renowned a musician as the great genius, Paderewski? Look for a circle at the top of your palm, between the third and fourth fingers. This circle may express itself either in composition or brilliant technique in playing any musical instrument. It is always seen in the hands of great singers. The circle is clearly shown in Paderewski's hand, and is known as THE CIRCLE OF MUSICAL GENIUS.

Ignace Jan Paderewski was born in Kurilowa, Russian Poland. His rare genius first evidenced itself at the age of 3, and at the age of 7 he was given his first lessons, studying piano composition later in Berlin. At the age of 23 he made his triumphant first public appearance in Vienna, and since then he has enchanted his audiences the world over. Through the years the nations of the world have acclaimed the great master. His technique has been the marvel of the musical world, and the charm and feeling he develops in his work never fail to inspire his audiences. The world has seen him, too, in a passionate fight for Poland's independence, and in 1919 as the first Premier of the new Poland. In 1927 he returned to the concert stage.

Page 73

EAMON de VALERA

LOOK AT YOUR HAND

DOES your hand show the line of determined purpose which characterizes that of Eamon de Valera, President of the Irish Free State? Look for a line beginning on the side of the hand underneath the first finger, touching slightly the line of life, and running straight across the palm. This line is clearly depicted in De Valera's hand and signifies boundless energy and a daring, self-sacrificing determination of purpose. It is known as THE LINE OF UNDAUNTED DETERMINATION.

Ireland's stormy petrel, destined for historic fame as one of Erin's greatest patriots, was born in New York in 1880 of a Spanish father and an Irish mother. He returned early to Ireland for his education, and interested himself in the Irish independence movement in 1913. As leader of the Extremists, he first came to world attention during the Easter Rebellion of 1916. He was a constant thorn in England's side from then on until 1922, when the Dail Eireann ratified the peace treaty with Great Britain which resulted in the founding of the Irish Free State. Then he rebelled against the government accepted by Ireland and resigned as President of the Sinn Fein Parliament. He has never ceased his agitation for absolute independence, although he and his followers swore allegiance to the King of England. "An empty political formality having no binding significance," he called that oath to which he swore, in his determination to enter the Dail Eireann as an opponent of the Free State. To him and his constituents the oath to the King means that the Free State is included in the British Commonwealth of Nations. His purpose is independence to establish Ireland as the equal of England and other nations. In 1932 he was elected President of the Free State.

LOOK AT YOUR HAND

JANE ADDAMS

ARE you, like Jane Addams, destined to become noted for one of the highest characteristics human beings can have—a deep and unselfish interest in humanity? Look for a line starting under the fourth finger on the side of the hand, passing across the hand and ending in a fork, one branch of which is below the index finger and the other between this and the second finger. This line, clearly seen in Jane Addams' hand, indicates capability of any, even the greatest, sacrifice for the sake of humanity. It is known as THE LINE OF DEEP HUMAN SYMPATHY.

No life could better exemplify this sign than that of the great pioneer social service worker, which she has given entirely to a crusade for the betterment of social conditions. Jane Addams' father was a public-spirited man and intimate friend of Abraham Lincoln. Undoubtedly Lincoln's great ideals and fight for the downtrodden, and her father's practical humanitarian ideas, have influenced her so deeply that to lighten the burden of the poor, lowly and forgotten became the controlling idea of her life. Her "Hull House" settlement in the slums of Chicago is a memorial to her untiring efforts—it is the most widely known social settlement in the world. One of the foremost pacifists of our time, she was awarded the Noble Peace Prize in 1931 for her untiring, unselfish work for world peace. For that all-embracing, self-forgetting love which has marked her life, she is identified as one of the greatest Americans.

LOOK AT YOUR HAND

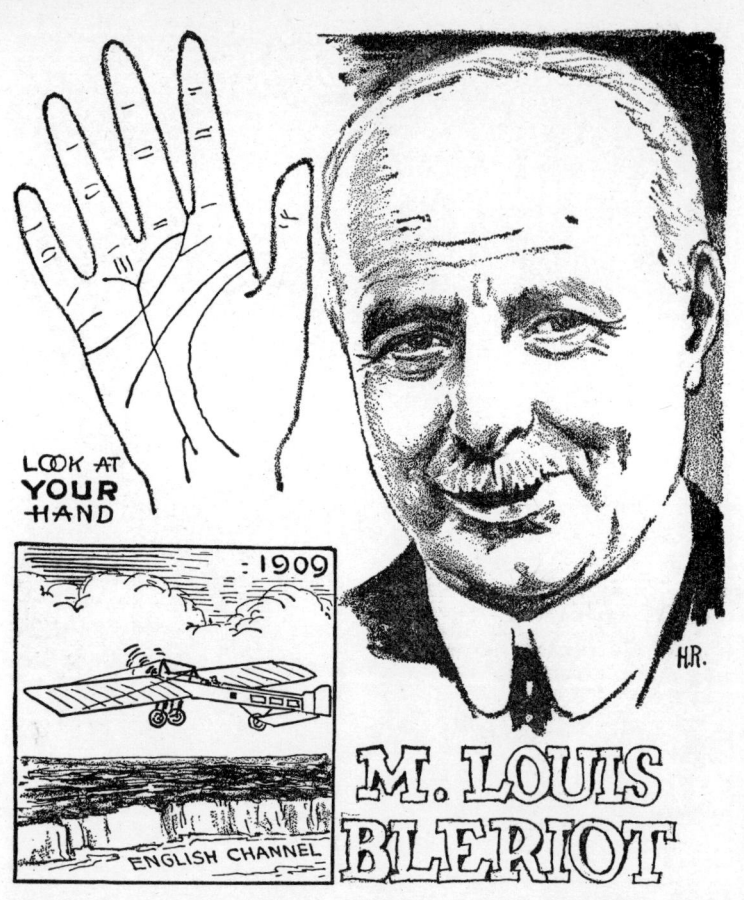

M. LOUIS BLERIOT

ARE you destined to become a mechanical genius like Louis Bleriot, pioneer of aviation and France's greatest contributor to the science of flight? Look for a semicircle underneath your middle finger. This sign is clearly shown in Louis Bleriot's hand and signifies an aptitude for supreme skill in mechanics. It is known as THE SEMICIRCLE OF MECHANICAL GENIUS.

This French pioneer of aviation, who made his first flight—albeit of only six seconds' duration—in 1907 in a machine of his own design, was destined for a monumental achievement two years later. It was then that his first flight across the English Channel made aviation history. Though disabled by burns and without compass or navigating instruments, this French trail-blazer astonished the world with his then incredible feat. He still lives, having survived nearly a hundred accidents, to marvel at the transformation which time and experimentation have wrought in the science of aviation to which his own genius gave such epochal significance a quarter of a century ago. The evolution of the slow, fragile open planes of his heyday to the fast, sturdy machines of the modern era must have given Louis Bleriot great satisfaction through these astounding years.

Page 76

LOOK AT **YOUR** HAND

KING ALBERT OF BELGIUM

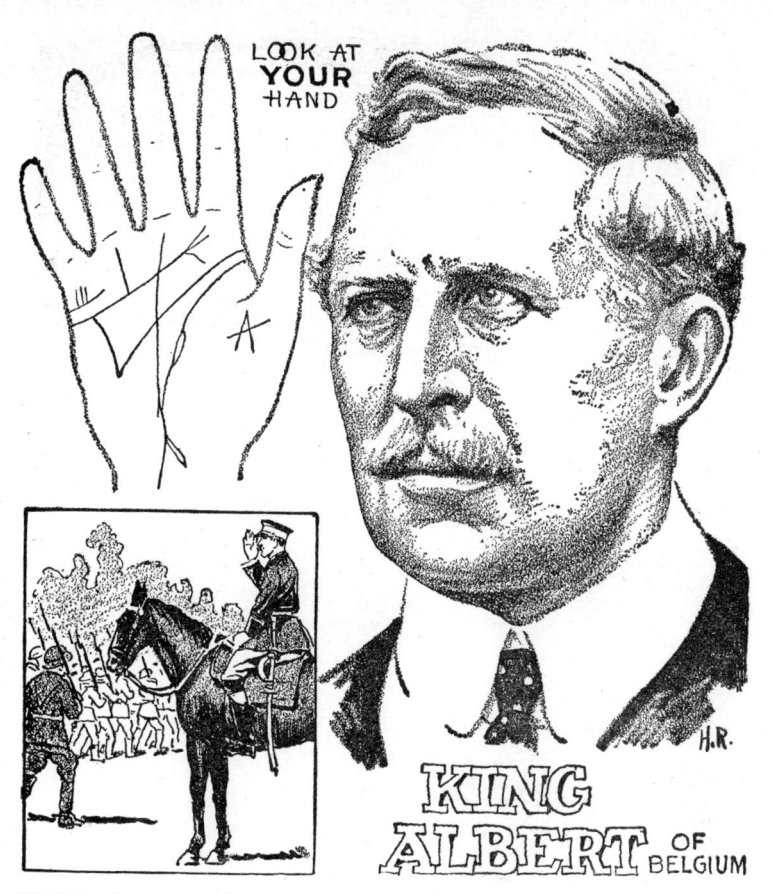

How does your hand compare with that of King Albert of Belgium? Look for a quadrangle in the center of the palm, a rough square formed by the three major lines of heart, destiny and head, and a line closing these at the side of the hand. This quadrangle is clearly seen in King Albert's hand, pictured above, and denotes a generous nature and indomitable spirit. It is always in the hands of sincere leaders of liberal thought.

It is for the qualities indicated by this quadrangle that the monarch of the Belgians, born in 1875 and married to a German princess, has come to be recognized as the hardest worker among European royalty, one of the greatest democratic rulers of our time, a good soldier, engineer and writer. It is undoubtedly largely to his fortitude that history will accredit the saving of Paris during the World War. His talents, his grasp of the actualities of the campaign, his clear understanding of field strategy and the high order of his moral leadership were such that he was able to hold back the German advance into France. And such is his democratic understanding nature that he is beloved and respected by his people, perhaps more than any other reigning monarch. There is a story that is still believed, that Albert in his younger days, when he was not yet married, adventured through the United States in hobo fashion for the experience of seeing the common people and America at close range—another version is that he worked as a reporter on a certain Eastern paper. Generally speaking, the possessor of the quadrangle has an open mind and broad view, combined with a democratic attitude toward his fellow men.

Page 77

LOOK AT YOUR HAND

MUSTAPHA KEMAL PASHA

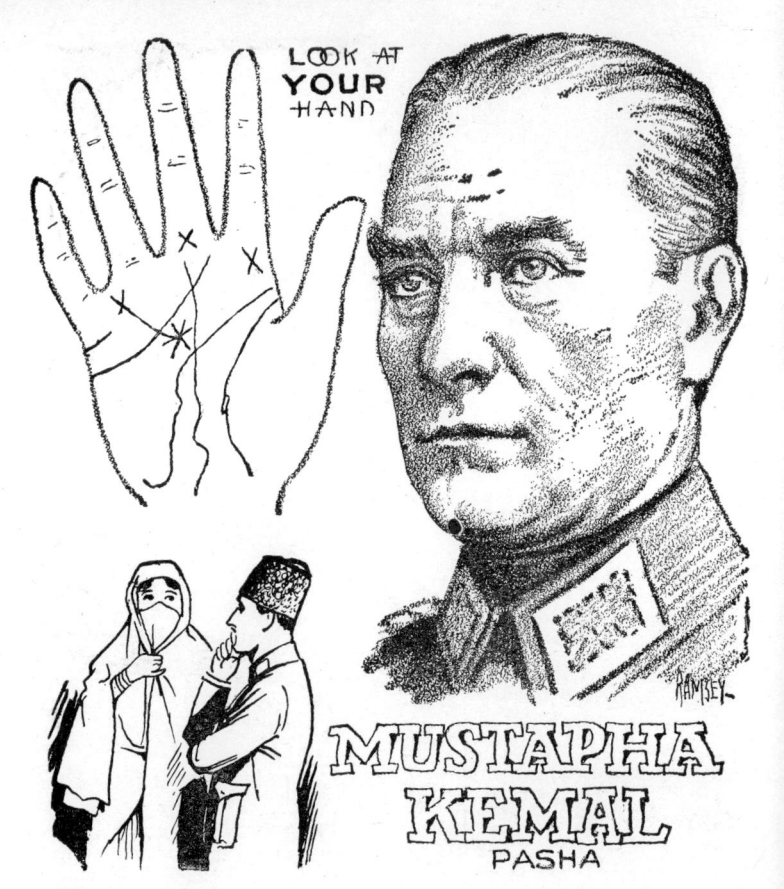

HAVE you, like Mustapha Kemal, creator and President of the Turkish Republic, the kind of will power that conquers every obstacle? Look in your hand; if you see a star in the center of your palm between the lines of head and heart, you have a personality that, by sheer power of relentless will, conquers everything that stands in its way. This rare sign is clearly shown in Kemal's hand. It is called THE STAR OF THE CONQUEROR.

Mustapha Kemal, modernizer of Turkey, decided upon a military career at an early age and at the age of 24 was promoted to the rank of captain. Some time later, he led the Young Turk revolt to depose Sultan Abdul Hamid, "The Damned." His real opportunity came during the World War, when he won high recognition through his brilliant defense of Gallipoli. He bitterly opposed the Treaty of Versailles and immediately declared Turkish independence of allied control in Constantinople. In 1920 he seized power from the Sultan. In a series of brilliantly executed maneuvers he forced the Greeks out of Asia Minor and Smyrna and banished the Sultan from Constantinople—abolishing at the same time the Caliphate, or religious supremacy of the Sultan, over the entire Moslem world—and adopted the social code of the West. Kemal is justly hailed as the "Father of the Country" by the Turks, and was given the title "Ghazi" or "Conqueror." In 1923 he was elected President of the Republic and immediately inaugurated a social revolt unparalleled in the history of the world, bringing Turkey out of its medieval stupor, abolishing the fez and the harem, scrapping Arabic writing for the Latin alphabet, and converting the republic into a modern state.

LOOK AT **YOUR** HAND

GEN. CHARLES G. DAWES

WILL your ability to concentrate bring you success? This is one of the outstanding characteristics of General Dawes, whose hand clearly shows the line indicating such powers. Look for the line which starts at the side of the hand under the first finger and runs across the palm, slightly curving at the end. It denotes a striking ability to concentrate on the thing at hand and is known as THE LINE OF PROFOUND CONCENTRATION.

This outstanding member of American public life has shown throughout his career a vigor and outspokenness which have given him his famous sobriquet, "Hell 'n' Maria" Dawes. Born in Ohio in 1865, the son of Brigadier General Rufus R. Dawes, commander of the Iron Brigade of Wisconsin in the Civil War, he studied law. In Nebraska, where he took up his law practice, he became one of the leading barristers of the State. Success has marked his entire career, which has embraced not only law, but politics, finance, soldiering, diplomacy and the arts. During the war he distinguished himself as general purchasing agent for the American Expeditionary Forces as well as for his activities as a member of the Military Board of Allied Supply, for which he was decorated by both France and the United States. He first gained political attention as a member of the Republican National Committee. His election as Vice President to Coolidge followed, after which he was appointed by Hoover as Ambassador to England. Proficiency has been his middle name, not only in public life but in authorship and music.

Page 79

LOOK AT YOUR HAND

DOUGLAS FAIRBANKS

HAVE you the abounding energy which has so amazed the world in Douglas Fairbanks, Sr.? If you have you should be able to find a line in your hand, inside the Line of Life opposte the thumb, like that clearly outlined in Fairbanks' hand, illustrated above. It denotes exceptional vitality and enthusiasm and is known as THE LINE OF VITALITY.

The athletic prowess of this popular screen actor is clearly exemplified in his cinema portrayals. He put a certain zip into films that set him individually apart. His fondness for golf, tennis and other sports is well known. Even now he shows unusual energy and enthusiasm. He was born in Denver, Col., in 1884. From his father he acquired a great love of Shakespeare and became quite a Shakespearean scholar. He naturally turned to the stage and when plans did not materialize successfully at first he jumped into various sorts of work in turn: studied mining, clerked in a bond house, worked in a hardware store, took up the study of law—with the same "get up and go" that has marked his entire life. He always came back to the stage, but from his entry into films his career took him up the ladder of success by leap and bounds, literally and figuratively. One has only to recall "The Three Musketeers," "The Thief of Bagdad" and other films through which he hop-skip-and-jumped with that infectious smile.

LOOK AT YOUR HAND

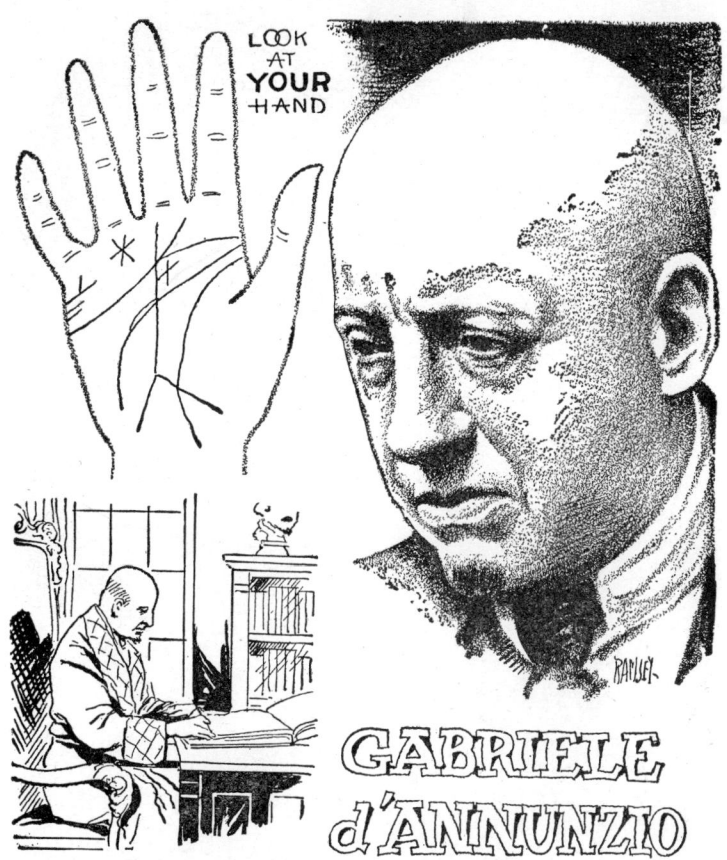

GABRIELE d'ANNUNZIO

ARE you destined to have a romantic career, like Gabriele d'Annunzio, brilliant poet and writer and the national hero of Italy? Look for two lines at the bottom of your palm, beginning on either side of your hand and joining the line of destiny. These lines, clearly seen in D'Annunzio's hand, indicate a career likely to abound in adventure, romance and turbulent passion. They are called THE LINES OF ROMANCE.

The great genius and lover, D'Annunzio, was born in 1863 to become a national hero of his native Italy. Ardor has marked his entire career, which began with poetic and literary works in his teens. Entering journalism in Rome, he pursued his writings, which have given to the world such works as "La Giocanda," "The Dead City," "The Flame of Life" and many other noted books. His love affair with the great Eleanora Duse will always live in memory, for both are among the Italian immortals. In 1915 the fiery romanticist turned patriot. His eloquence led Italy into the World War, in which his aviation achievements were daring. The most dramatic undertaking of his life followed the Armistice, when the Allies refused to give the great Adriatic port, Fiume, to Italy. Defying peace agreements and his own Government, D'Annunzio successfully led volunteer raiders on the city, which they held until 1920. Forced to relinquish Fiume, he retired. But Italy retained that city. Since then his life has been secluded in 1924 he was made Prince of Montenevoso, a tribute to his patriotism and valor.

LOOK AT YOUR HAND

EVANGELINE BOOTH

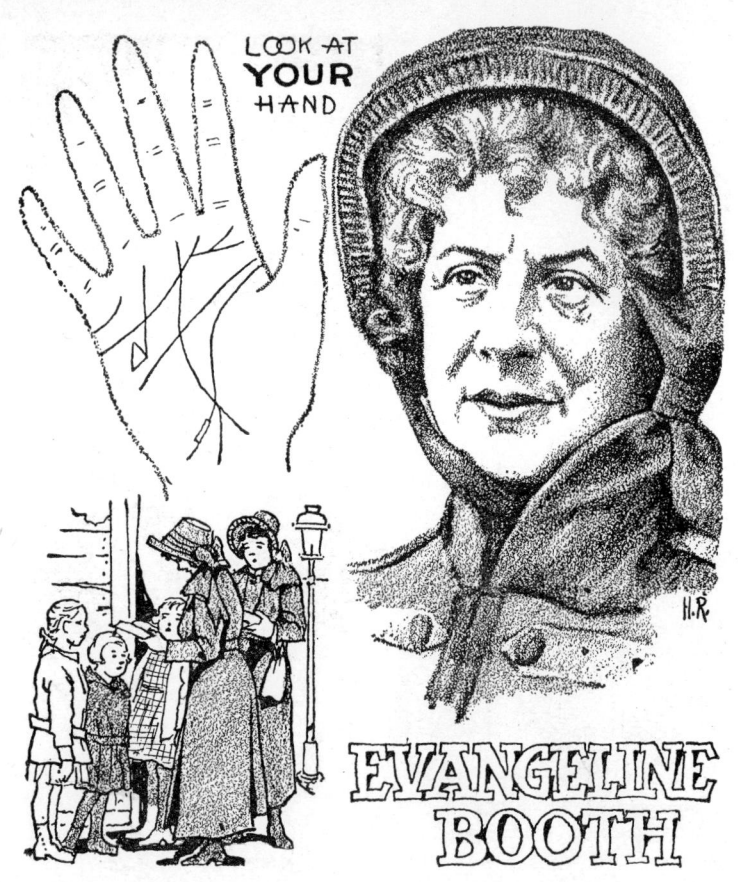

ARE you destined to become noted for your great heart and vigorous leadership, like Evangeline Booth, commander-in-chief of the Salvation Army in the United States? If your heart line begins on the side of your hand underneath your fourth finger and runs across your palm, ending in a fork with one branch underneath the first finger and the other between the first and second fingers, you have the greatness of heart and the militant leadership which made Commander Booth's career possible. This is THE LINE OF HEART.

Evangeline Cory Booth has given her entire life to the saving of human bodies and souls—the great work of the Salvation Army which was founded by her father, General William Booth. In command of the American branch of that great army of social workers and soul redeemers since 1904, she is an untiring worker who does not count the hours of the day she is spending on her work on the streets, in prisons, at meetings and in the training of rookies to carry on the good word. During the Wold War, Commander Booth sent a small convoy of her own to the battlefields in Europe, and to this day the warm-hearted Salvationists' service, catering to the spiritual and physical comfort of the troops, is remembered by the veterans. Her great zeal for leadership, and her ability for it, have set her apart as one of the greatest benefactresses of the age. I have seen this line in the hands of outstanding social workers who dedicate their lives to public service and, while everybody has a heart line, the forks underneath the index and second finger are the significant signs to look for.

Page 82

LOOK AT **YOUR** HAND

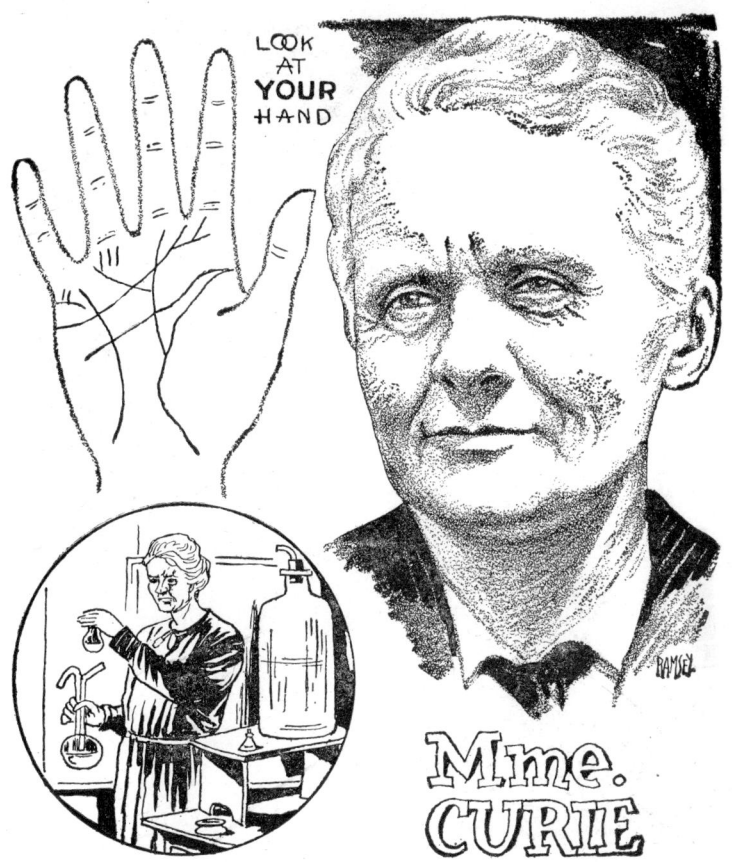

Mme. CURIE

HAVE you, like Mme. Marie Curie, co-discoverer with her husband of radium and polonium, the sixth sense which enables you to divine things despite the lack of ordinary evidence? If you have, you may be able to find a line in your hand, starting below the fourth finger on the side of your hand and taking a course in semicircular form down your palm. This line is clearly seen in Mme. Curie's hand. It denotes a highly intuitive mind, which enables its possessors to solve sometimes baffling problems, where the keenest minds had been vainly searching for a solution. It is called THE LINE OF INTUITION.

Mme. Curie was born in Warsaw, Poland, on November 7, 1867, and received her early scientific training from her father, Dr. Sklodowska. She became involved in a student's revolutionary organization, and it was advisable for her to leave Warsaw. Settling in Paris, she became the world's most famous woman scientist, and, with her husband, Pierre Curie, discovered radium and polonium. In 1903 they jointly received the Davy medal and in the same year the Nobel Prize. Prof. Curie was accidentally killed. Mme. Curie succeeded him as professor at the Paris University. The Nobel Prize was awarded to her for chemistry in 1911. In recognition of her scientific work, the women of America presented her with a gram of the precious metal she had discovered, and later on American friends contributed $50,000 toward the purchase of radium for her Warsaw laboratory. She personally directs the Curie Radium Institute, built by the French Government in Paris, where she works diligently in her laboratories, seeking new scientific benefits for mankind.

LOOK AT YOUR HAND

GUGLIELMO MARCONI

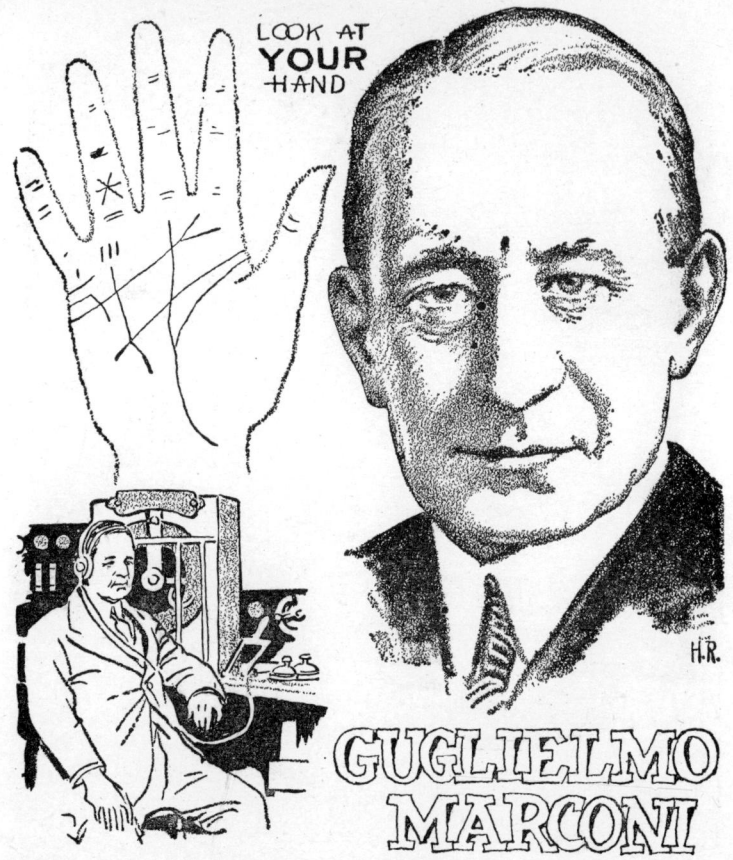

DOES your hand show that you are gifted along scientific lines? Perhaps, like Guglielmo Marconi, famous scientist and inventor of wireless telegraphy, you have the three short lines at the top of your palm between the third and fourth fingers, which portray a keen analytical mind and a great ability in scientific research.

Senator Marconi, son of an Italian father and an Irish mother, first carried out his experiments in connection with wireless telegraphy at Bologna University. In 1896 he went to England and in that year took out the first patent ever granted for wireless telegraphy based on the use of electric waves. The following year he set up communication with battleships twelve miles out to sea. By 1898 he had established wireless communication across the English Channel, and by 1901 across the Atlantic. Six years later he put into operation the first public wireless service between England and America. In 1909 he received the Nobel Prize for Physics. He had worked out the principles governing the so-called Hertzian wave, and his genius had transmuted what had been only a little understood phenomenon into one of man's most powerful instruments. He brought the world closer together than even steam has done; he made the great radio industry possible, and the lives saved at sea because of his invention are innumerable. In 1916 he began his work with very short waves, looking toward the development of the beam system of wireless communication. He has carried on this phase of his experimentation ever since, with increasingly successful results. Besides the Nobel Prize, he has been honored with the Albert Medal of the Royal Society of Arts, the Franklin and John Fritz medals and many others.

Page 84

LOOK AT YOUR HAND

PLUTARCO ELIAS CALLES

ARE you, like General Plutarco Elias Calles, strong man of Mexico, a natural leader? Look for a star underneath your first finger. This sign is clearly shown in General Calles' hand and signifies the born leader of men. It is called THE STAR OF POWERFUL LEADERSHIP.

One of the few living ex-Presidents of turbulent Mexico, Calles rose to power from very humble beginnings. Born in 1877 of lowly parentage, he eagerly educated himself so that by the time he was 17 he became a school teacher. Coming of age, he was made superintendent of schools in his native city, Hermosillo. Restlessness led him into political life, first in the Carranza revolt against Huerta; then with Obregon two years later in his campaign against Villa. This latter began a partnership which eventuated in Obregon and Calles establishing themselves as leaders of modern Mexico. After serving in the Cabinets of both Carranza and Obregon, Calles himself was elected President. His brilliancy, sincerity and tremendous force of character, coupled with inborn qualities of leadership, mark him as the only self-made man to rise to the office of Chief Executive of Mexico in an era of violent transitions. His is not a career founded on bloodshed. Rather, it is largely due to his practice of equity and restraint that Mexico has found a new spirit.

LOOK AT YOUR HAND

VICKI BAUM

WILL you reach the goal you have set for yourself, like Vicki Baum, author of "Grand Hotel?" Look at the base of your first finger for a cross, which indicates that you are likely to attain long-cherished ambitions. It is known as THE CROSS OF FULFILLED AMBITIONS.

This sign has brought international fame to the gifted Viennese writer but fame in a quite different guise from that to which she aspired in girlhood. Music was her first forte, but it had always been her ambition to be an author. At eighteen she married a young writer who could never finish his stories, so she wrote them for him, and they were published under his name. She divorced him finally and married Richard Lert, conductor of the State Opera of Berlin. The devastating flood of the afterwar inflation swept away their little fortune, and she was forced to plunge seriously into writing as editor of "Die Dame" (The Lady), and as a novelist. She wrote two novels which found a large reading public. Then came "Menschen in Hotel" from her prolific pen to become the internationally sensational "Grand Hotel" which shot her to world-wide acclaim. Well under 40 years of age, Vicki Baum already basks in the reflection of fulfilled ambitions and continues to write with the keen observation and analytical mind that has done so much toward establishing that success. In other cases the meaning of this cross may be changed by the modification through the rest of the lines so as to indicate over-ambition, love to dominate, excessive pride, etc.

Page 86

LOOK AT YOUR HAND

WINSTON CHURCHILL

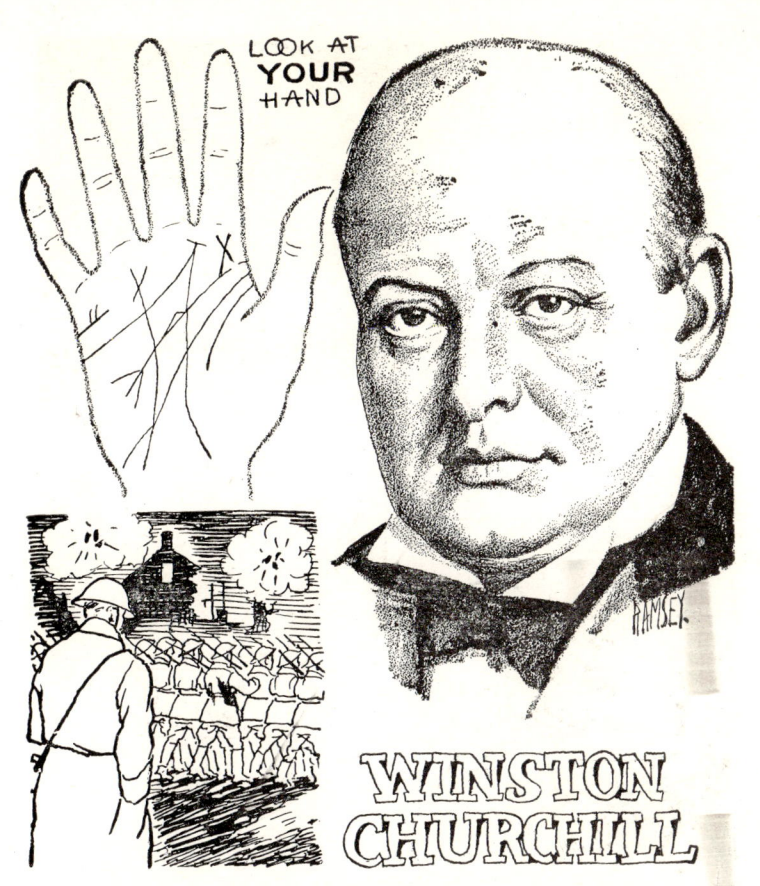

HAVE you confidence in your own opinions, despite others' dissent? If you find a cross underneath your first finger, sending out a branch to what is known as the line of head, you probably have great self-confidence, sometimes verging on a superiority complex. This cross is clearly seen in Winston Churchill's hand. It is known as THE CROSS OF DOMINEERING CHACTERISTICS

It was obvious from his aristocratic birth in 1874, as the eldest son of Lord Randolph Churchill, that Winston Churchill's destiny was to be coupled with that of his native England. As statesman, politician, author and soldier, his record bears out that destiny. His sense of humor, eloquence and resourcefulness caused him to rise rapidly in politics, which he entered by election to the House of Commons in 1901. In 1908 he first became a member of the Cabinet and, with short intervals, he has continued as leading member of the British Government. As First Lord of the Admiralty he figured prominently at the outset of the World War. After the Armistice, he undertook to write a series of books on his own views of the war from the vantage points of the War Room in the Admiralty, from the Ministry of Ammunition, and from the observer's seat of a fighting airplane. "The World Crisis," in four volumes, marks the peak of his literary career.

Page 87

LOOK AT YOUR HAND

NICETO ALCALA ZAMORA

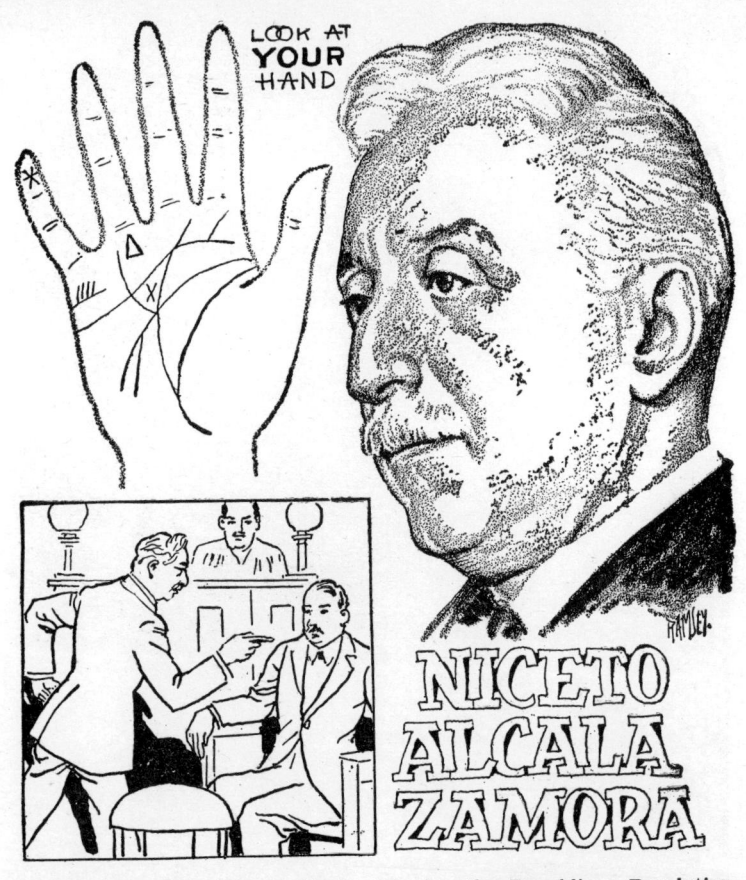

HAVE you, like Niceto Alcala-Zamora, first President of the newly formed Spanish Republic, the power to sway men by words alone? Look for a star at the top of your fourth finger, for this sign denotes a power of eloquence which, by its fiery passion, seldom fails to carry away its audiences. It is known as THE STAR OF FIERY ELOQUENCE.

The first President of Spain following the fall of the royal regime, was born of Andalusian stock. For many years an ardent monarchist he swung over to republicanism with Primo de Rivera's dictatorship. It was largely due to Zamora's zeal that King Alfonso's downfall occurred. Imprisoned for signing the Republican Revolutionary Manifesto in 1930, and charged with high treason, Zamora emerged to assume the presidency, following in his family's traditions of liberalism, which date back to 1812 in Spain's political history. It was he, who, freed from his prison cell, ordered the departure from Spain of the royal family. On his shoulders he now bears the weight of his country's destiny. The political troubles which harass his regime have been numerous, but he has made his way among them, so far successfully, with an inborn tact, diplomacy and sound common sense.

Page 88

LOOK AT **YOUR** HAND

ALFRED E. SMITH

ARE you, like Alfred E. Smith, one of the best-known Governors New York ever had, a born executive? If so, you should be able to find a triangle in the center of your hand, below the middle finger. This triangle, which indicates great executive powers, is clearly seen in "Al" Smith's hand. It is known as **THE TRIANGLE OF BRILLIANT ADMINISTRATIVE ABILITY.**

Alfred E. Smith's political genius catapulted him from his famous sidewalks of New York to the governorship of the Empire State and presidential candidacy. His is a classical example of American democracy—of what America means to a man with a will to succeed and a sound brain to direct a good right arm. "Al," as he is familiarly called by all who know him, was born in the old Fourth Ward in New York City on December 30, 1873. His parents were poor and the family lived in the Irish colony under the Brooklyn Bridge. His father died when he was quite young and he had to leave school to help support the family. He found work in the Fulton Fish Market as a checker, where he remained for seven years. He began his political career in 1895 and became an Assemblyman. He ran for Governor in 1918 and is the first man in the State to have the honor of being Governor for four terms. The story of "Al" Smith's life has become part of the history of present-day America and there is little need to enlarge upon it here. If any man has shown a genius for administrative work in a long public career, that has remained particularly free from scandal or suspicion of any sort, it is that of this fine citizen of the United States.

Page 89

LOOK AT **YOUR** HAND

MOHANDAS K. GANDHI

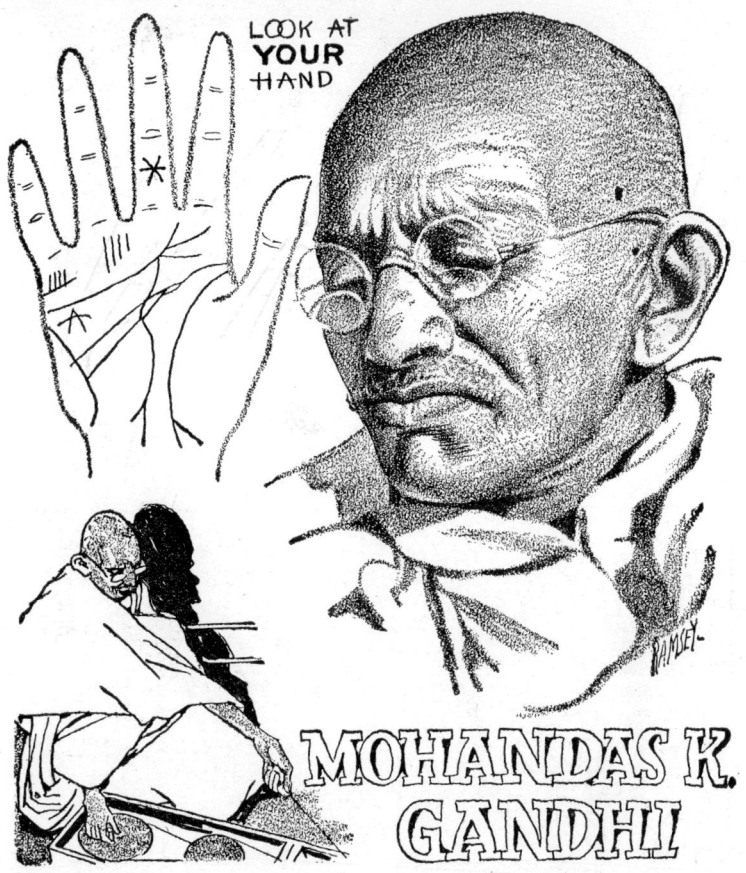

HAVE you the sign of great wisdom in your hand? Look for a triangle formed by three lines in the center of your palm. This triangle is clearly shown in the illustration of Gandhi's hand, and his life is proof of the fact that it gives to its possessor a superhuman wisdom and a moral strength which transcends mere physical force. This is THE TRIANGLE OF WISDOM.

Mohandas Karamchand Gandhi, the Mahatma, or "Great Soul" of India, has the wisdom of passive resistance and the strength to carry it out, as he struggles valiantly for the independence of his people, and the obliteration of the caste system that made millions "untouchables," outcasts forced to a life of abject misery. Time and again the British authorities have thrown him into prison for his demonstrations, but still they have grudgingly been grateful to the Mahatma for his advocacy and enforcement of non-violent resistance. The power which he has attained has resulted from his extraordinary self-effacement. He holds that peace and love will solve all problems, and he is resolved to do all in his power to make love a practical force in this world. His hand clearly shows the lines of imperial conquest, yet his indomitable will directs his destiny, and he cares only for the power necessary to relieve his millions of followers from the inhuman caste system.

Page 90

LOOK AT YOUR HAND

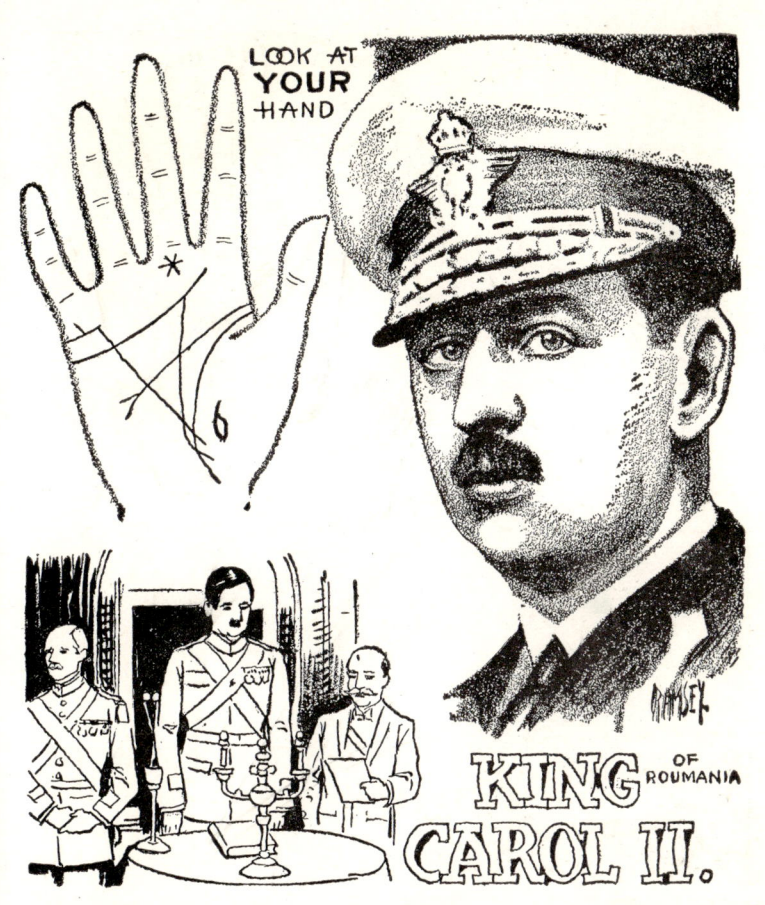

KING CAROL II. OF ROUMANIA

DO YOUR moods change rapidly? Perhaps, like King Carol of Rumania, you have what is called an "island" on your palm, located underneath the base of the thumb. This island is plainly apparent in King Carol's hand, illustrated above. It denotes changeable moods and affections inclined to go to extremes in all things, and is known as THE ISLAND OF TROUBLED INFATUATION.

King Carol the Second, who returned to his native Rumania to take the throne he renounced when a pretty face, a pair of flashing eyes and two rosebud lips proved more appealing than a kingdom, bears out the saying that "uneasy lies the heart when the head wears a crown." King Carol's young life was full of turbulent love affairs. By nature gay and reckless, he is a product of his environment and inheritance. He grew up surrounded by the deep political conspiracies and romantic intrigue of the Balkans, where marriages are made for political reasons and love goes roaming anywhere. With his holiday over and his tempestuous career steadied by the weight of more mature years, Carol came back to Rumania, and only time will tell whether he will be able to control his urges for more romantic adventures.

Page 91

LOOK AT YOUR HAND

EX-PRESIDENT HERBERT HOOVER

HAVE you the ability to become a successful engineer, like Herbert Hoover? Look for three short lines underneath the third finger, like those clearly shown in the illustration of ex-President Hoover's hand. These lines denote great success as a result of engineering genius. They are known as THE LINES OF ENGINEERING GENIUS.

The triangle seen in the center of Hoover's palm denotes great administrative ability. This Iowa farm boy, born in 1874, has left his record of success on the pages of not only the United States but world history. At 25 he was earning $15,000 yearly with his engineering activities, which later took him to England, China and other countries in the interests of mining. In 1914 he sprang into public prominence by directing the credit and transportation activities necessary to return 200,000 stranded Americans from Europe at the outbreak of the World War. His organization and administration of Belgian war relief and successful efforts as Food Administrator under President Wilson are a matter of record. His fight now was against famine, plagues and destitution. One of his most notable achievements was that of relief in the Mississippi River flood of 1917, when he was Secretary of Commerce. The resulting low mortality and relative freedom from sickness among the refugees in the stricken area were ascribed in great part to his experience in Belgian relief and to his gifts as an organizer. He reached the pinnacle of his career in the election of 1928, which made him President.

Page 92

LOOK AT YOUR HAND

HELEN WILLS MOODY

CAN you do more than one thing exceptionally well? If so, you may be able to find lines commencing at the side of your hand under the first finger and running across your palm, dividing toward the end into two branches, one slightly curving upward, the other branch curving downward. This sign is clearly shown in the illustration of Helen Wills Moody's hand, and shows a versatile nature. It is called **THE LINES OF VERSATILITY**.

The upward curve of Mrs. Moody's line denotes her perfect mental and muscular co-ordination manifesting itself in her marvelous tennis playing. The other branch, curving downward, signifies a marked artistic ability that finds expression in music or, as in Mrs. Moody's case, art. When she was 15 she secured the American Girls' tennis championship. In 1923 she beat Mrs. Mallory and Miss McKane and won the United States singles, retaining the title during the next two years. This was the beginning of a long list of triumphs. Though defeated by Suzanne Lenglen, the great French player, in 1926, she managed to give her the fright of her life. Marriage in 1929 to Frederick S. Moody, San Francisco stock broker, did not end her career. By 1932 she had won the United States championship seven times and the Wimbledon and French titles four times each. Placid, she is also endowed with great strength. With speed she combines accuracy, and she has developed all sides of her play. She is never ruffled or excited during the most critical stages of a match, and never either underrates or overrates an opponent. In addition to tennis she draws and paints portraits and landscapes and in the midst of her matchplaying found time for sketching.

LOOK AT YOUR HAND

Mme. MAGDA LUPESCU

HAVE you a tremendous attraction for the opposite sex? Perhaps, like Magda Lupescu, the woman who caused King Carol of Rumania to renounce his throne, you have a star underneath the base of your thumb, lying to one side of the hand. This star signifies irresistible attraction to the opposite sex, with extradorinary success in affairs of love. It is called THE STAR OF IRRESISTIBLE SEX MAGNETISM.

Since the art of speech began, a favorite sport of novelist and dramatist has been the analysis of that peculiar charm which famous sirens of history have wielded over kings, generals and other men of power. Mme. Lupescu is no doubt a woman of great allure, with red hair and camellia white skin. She is gay and vivacious companion, full of abounding energy, vitality and pep.

Page 94

H. G. WELLS

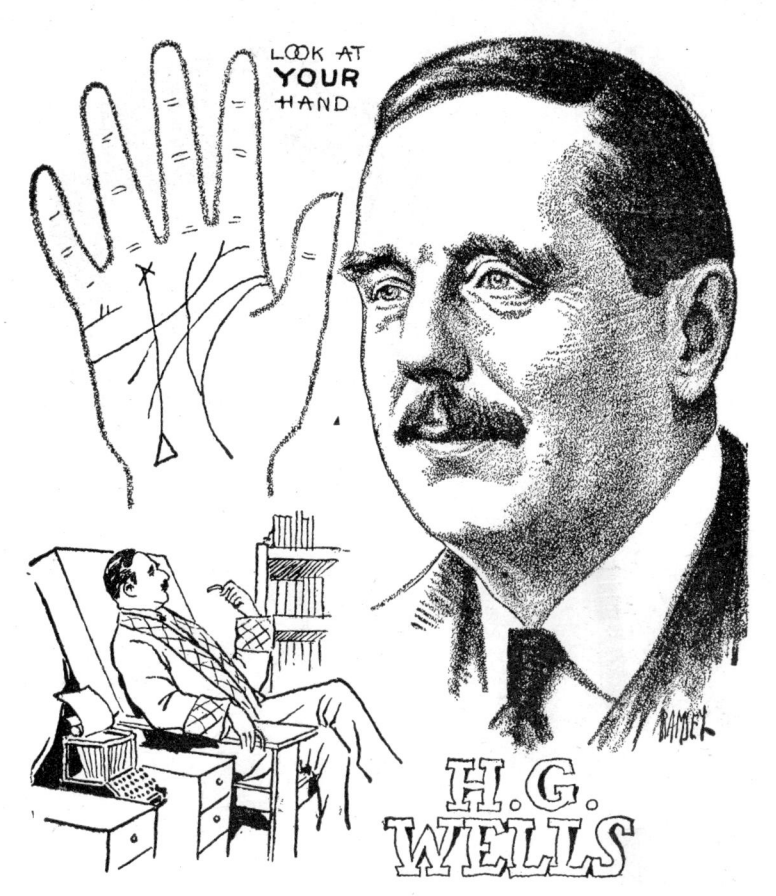

HAVE you, like H. G. Wells, the type of imagination which indulges in what seems like the wildest fantasy, yet which later proves to be, in part at least, a forecast of the future? Look for a triangle at the bottom of your palm underneath the fourth finger. This sign is clearly seen on H. G. Wells' hand, illustrated above, and denotes a faculty for flights of fancy which may carry in them grains of real prophetic truth. It is known as THE TRIANGLE OF PROPHETIC INTELLECT.

Wells, the great English author whose "Outline of History" marked the beginning of a new era in historical writing, was born in Kent in 1866. With a fine early education, he turned to science, and was graduated with honors in zoology from the Royal College of Science. Newspaper work then led him to write his first book, "The Time Machine," in 1895. Since then his prolific pen has turned out two or more books yearly. Although he has written more than sixty books, forty of which were fiction, he is best known for his "Outline of History," which many critics claim has had wider and more immediate influence on the public than any other twentieth century work in any language. He shares with Jules Verne the curious gift of making the wildest flights of imagination seem scientifically natural. Though keenly interested in public affairs, he has never actively participated in them, but his political and social ideas have exerted international influence. He has been said to have a vista of new worlds—an aim to quicken civilization.

Page 95

LOOK AT **YOUR** HAND

JACK DEMPSEY

ARE you a fighter, like Jack Dempsey? If so, you should be able to find a square underneath **your** first finger like the one plainly apparent in Dempsey's hand. This sign indicates superior physical stamina and the magnificent courage of a born fighter. It is called THE SQUARE OF THE BORN FIGHTER.

Jack Dempsey today as an ex-champion holds quite as many followers as he did when he was champion heavyweight boxer of the world. As a fighter he reveled in his trade and gloried in the glamour of his title. His life as a fighter was as colorful as the great ring melodramas in which he starred Even today he still looks like the most magnificent athlete that was ever born, but the fire has died down. The hard lines of the killer's face have softened and the spring has gone out of the most marvelous pair of limbs that ever were fastened to a human being.

Page 96

LOOK AT YOUR HAND

EX-PRESIDENT OF CUBA
GERARDO MACHADO

COULD you make a successful politician? Look for a triangle in the center of your hand. This triangle, denoting practical ability in political business, is clearly shown in the hand of Gerardo Machado, ex-President of the Cuban Republic, but in his hand the grille which is seen under the second finger indicates great difficulties as a result of a ruthlessly selfish nature. The triangle is known as **THE TRIANGLE OF ORGANIZING ABILITY.**

General Machado, former President of the Cuban Republic, was born at Santa Clara in 1871, the son of a sugar planter who, with other revolutionists, took up arms against Spain. When Cuba began her successful revolution in 1895, he enlisted with his father in the revolutionary army and was wounded several times. By profession a butcher and lacking an education, he nevertheless became a popular and successful politician of the new Republic, playing upon the patriotic sentiments of the people. In 1925 he was elected President for a four-year term. With his rise to power he shed the cloak of the unselfish patriot and "benefactor of the people" and revealed himself as an unscrupulous "hardboiled" exploiter of the people, ruthless in suppressing all opposition. In spite of the growing popular hatred of his person and Administration, he knew how to get and hold the support of big capital and how to get himself re-elected in 1929. The outbreak against his oppression swept him out of office in August, 1933.

LOOK AT **YOUR** HAND

LIONEL BARRYMORE

ARE you destined to become a great actor, like Lionel Barrymore? Look for a tripod on the side of your palm, underneath your fourth finger. This sign is plainly apparent in the illustration of Barrymore's hand, and signifies brilliant ability and outstanding success in the world of make-believe. It is called THE TRIPOD OF BRILLIANT DRAMATIC ABILITY.

Lionel Barrymore, recognized as one of the foremost actors of stage and screen, was born in Philadelphia, the son of Maurice and Georgia Drew Barrymore. He was educated in New York and studied dramatic art in Paris, where he also was considered more than ordinarily gifted along artistic and musical lines. It has been said of him that he might have achieved just as much fame as a painter or a concert pianist as he did by following the family tradition of becoming an actor. His stage career, in which he scored brilliant successes, began very early in his life, but he had the distinction of being one of the first noted figures on the stage to give the cinema serious attention, and of appearing for the first time in 1909 on a motion picture set to work with Mary Pickford. His following screen career has been conspicuous by its continuous success.

Page 98

LOOK AT YOUR HAND

JOAN CRAWFORD

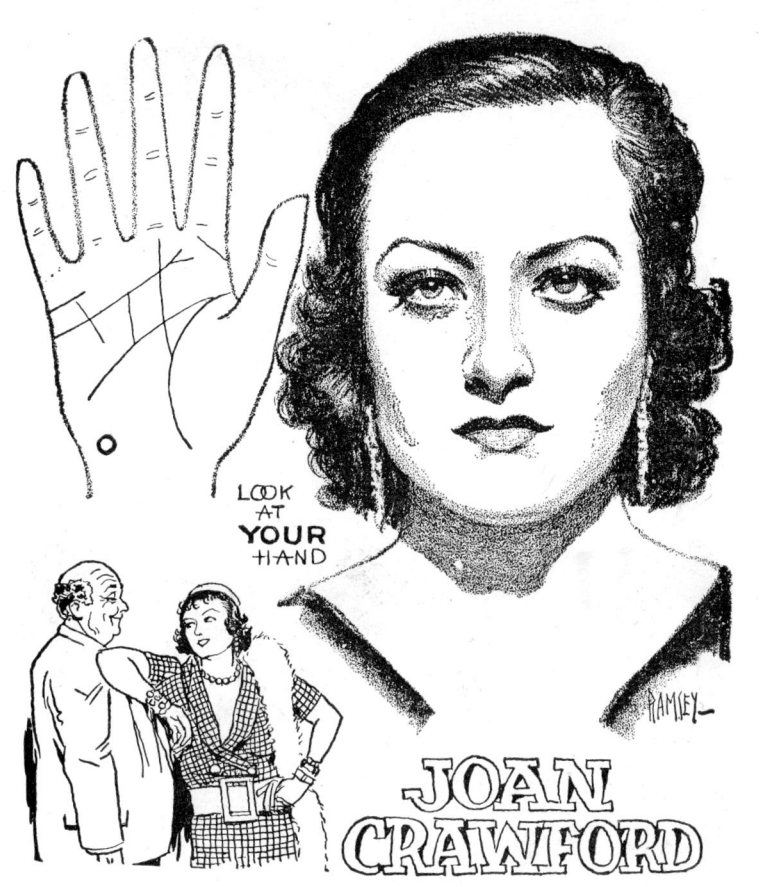

ARE you vividly imaginative and somewhat sensitive at the same time? Perhaps like Joan Crawford, you have a circle at the bottom of your palm near the wrist, which always indicates a vivid imagination and a somewhat sensitive nature. It is known as THE CIRCLE OF SENSITIVENESS.

Joan Crawford was born as Lucille Le Sueur in San Antonio, Tex., and acquired her present name in a magazine contest in which the fans were asked to rename the Miss Le Sueur, deemed too hard to remember and pronounce. She got the fever for the stage at an early age. Her father was a theatre owner. Despite their stage connections, however, the family opposed Joan's idea of a stage career, so she left home against their wishes and made her debut as a dancer in a Chicago revue. Later she came to New York and played in the "Passing Show" at the Winter Garden, where she attracted the attention of motion-picture producers, who brought her to California under contract.

LOOK AT **YOUR** HAND

SINCLAIR LEWIS

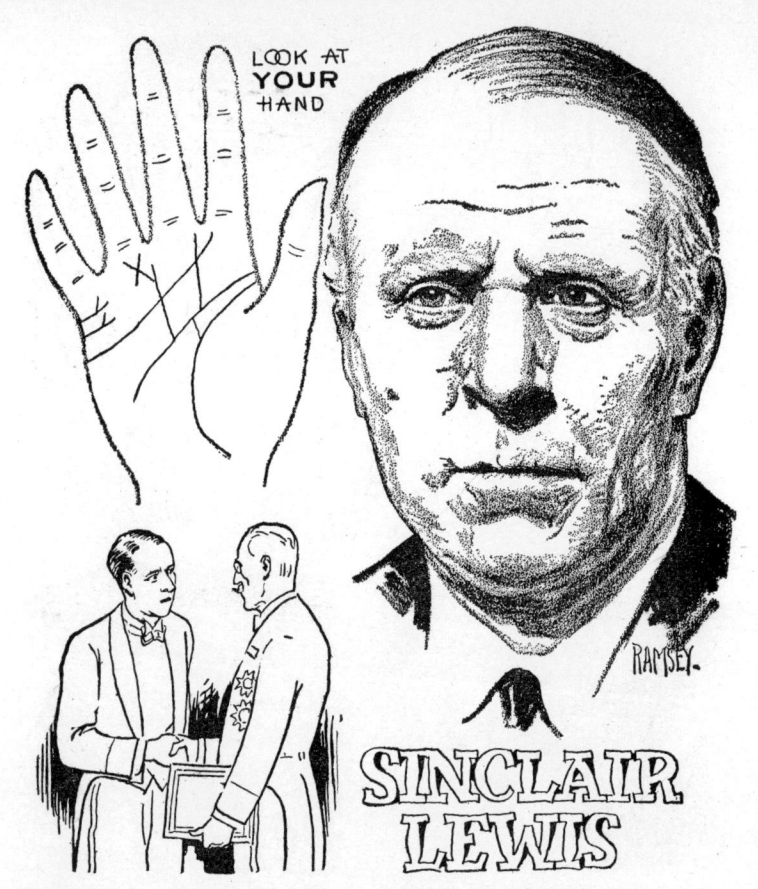

ARE you a keen observer, and can you put what you see into words? If so, like Sinclair Lewis, first American author to receive the Nobel Prize for Literature, you should be able to find a cross underneath your third finger. This sign denotes a keen sense of observation combined with the ability to put onto paper the things observed. It is known as THE CROSS OF KEEN OBSERVATION

Sinclair Lewis was born in Minnesota in 1885, of Connecticut stock descended from Welsh ancestors. At 7 he determined to be a writer, and, at 14, wrote his first story. But it was four years later before he found a market for his writings. After three years at Yale, he joined Upton Sinclair's Utopian Radical Colony in New Jersey as janitor of Helican Hall—a job which gave him plenty of time for writing. Thence he went to the gas house district of New York and, later, to complete his course at Yale. For many years he drifted about as reporter, reader, charity investigator and publicist. "Our Mr. Wrenn," his first novel, came out in 1914, to be followed by magazine editorship, short stories and more novels. A year's concentration turned out his famous "Main Street," the literary sensation of 1920. "Babbitt," "Elmer Gantry" and "Arrowsmith," in turn, won further recognition for his depth of understanding of human nature. The Nobel Prize award came in 1931. Contemporary American thought has been influenced considerably by his work, and he has added the word "Babbitt" to the language.

Page 100

LOOK AT **YOUR** HAND

CLARK GABLE

ARE you irresistibly attractive to the opposite sex? In other words, have you "IT"? If, like Clark Gable, adored of feminine movie fans, you have a line close to the bottom center of your palm, you have this attraction, and extraordinary success in all affairs of love. This sign is known as THE LINE OF "IT."

Clark Gable was born in Cadiz, O. He is six feet, one inch tall, has brown hair and gray eyes, and became interested in the stage through playing in little theatre productions. After playing some years in various stock companies, he became a star overnight for his portrayal in "The Last Mile." He tried several times to crash the movies, not very successfully, but finally succeeded in getting his first part in the picture "The Painted Desert" and from then on his popularity grew by leaps and bounds. Today he is no doubt one of the most popular and successful male stars on the screen.

LOOK AT YOUR HAND

LADY NANCY ASTOR

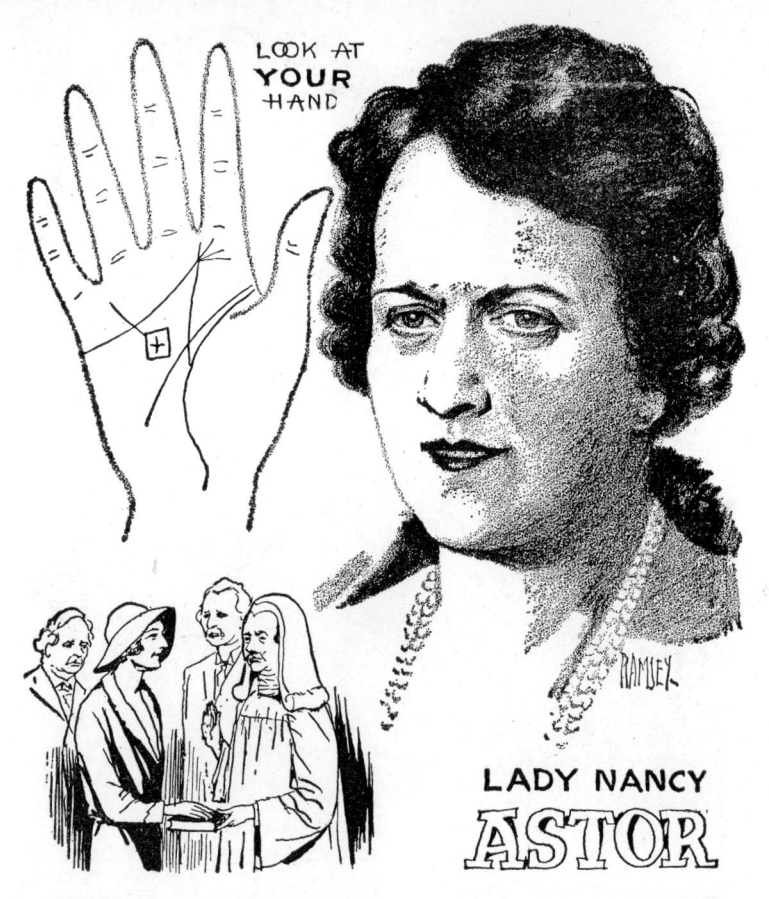

ARE you naturally religious, and perhaps a bit of a mystic as well? If so, like Lady Nancy Astor, first woman ever elected to the British Parliament, you may have a cross enclosed by a square in the center of your palm. This sign always denotes a person deeply religious and inclined toward mysticism. It is known as THE CROSS OF RELIGIOUS INSPIRATION.

This cross is the dominant feature in the palm of Lady Astor. Many people believe Lady Astor to be the most significant woman in England. She is famed for her originality and daring, and also for her fearless championship of temperance and social reforms, in defiance of powerful political interests. Lady Astor ascribes her career and phenomenal success to an early religious experience, and her political career dates from that day. Her palm plainly reveals that she is deeply religious.

Page 102

LOOK AT YOUR HAND

LORD READING

HAVE you the ability to become a successful lawyer? Look for four lines, extending from what is known as the line of head. These lines are clearly apparent in Lord Reading's hand and indicate an unusual aptitude for the law and legal processes. They are known as THE LINES OF JUDICIAL BRILLIANCY.

Of recent careers none approaches in romance, adventure and swift rise that of the present Marquess of Reading, the poor Jewish boy who rose to be Lord Chief Justice of England and Viceroy and Governor General of India. Born in 1860 as Rufus Daniel Isaacs, the son of a Jewish merchant in London, he rose to a career that almost overshadows that of the famous Disraeli. Running away to sea at 18, he returned to London to become a barrister at 27. Success and fortune marked his work to the extent that he was made British Attorney General at 50, Lord Chief Justice of England at 55 and special Ambassador to the United States in 1918. It is generally conceded that the financial policy which saved Great Britain from economic ruin at the outset of the World War was Lord Reading's. In 1921 he was appointed Viceroy and Governor General of India, a post which won him great popularity for his friendliness. For into the internal crisis of Gandhi's political revolt he brought a gracious but dominating personality. Although retired now from official duties, his genius still exerts great influence in world affairs.

Page 103

LOOK AT YOUR HAND

SENATOR WILLIAM E. BORAH

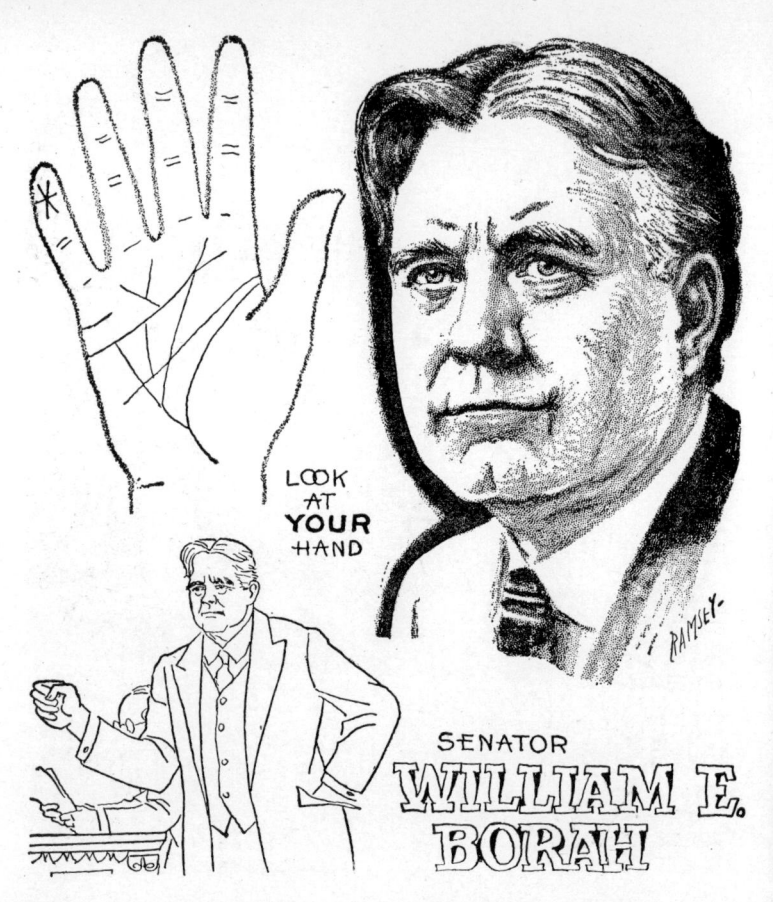

HAVE you the power to sway men by speech alone? Perhaps, like Senator William Edgar Borah, you have a star on the tip of your fourth finger. This star, apparent in the illustration of Borah's hand, denotes an oratorical genius and personal magnetism that never fails to impress listeners. It is known as THE STAR OF ELOQUENCE.

Senator Borah's long service in the United States Senate, which has won him a unique place in American public life, has borne witness to that genius and magnetism. Although a prominent member of the Progressive wing of the Republican Party, this fiery Senator from Idaho has refused to allow himself to be bound by party obligations. When he has the floor in the Senate his opponents listen as eagerly as his colleagues, for he always has something to say pro and con. An astute statesman, his vigirous criticism has helped often to sway administrative decisions. He supported the prosecution of the war with Germany, but opposed ratification of the Versailles Treaty. He opposed the Bonus Bill in 1924, and succeeded Lodge as chairman of the Foreign Relations Committee. So vigorous is he in his opinions and his fights for those opinions that he is one of the few American legislators known throughout the world not only as a statesman but for his activities in behalf of oppressed people as a humanitarian.

Page 104

LOOK AT YOUR HAND

RAYMOND POINCARÉ

ARE you a born diplomat? If so, you should be able to find three lines extending from your line of head, like those clearly shown in the illustration of the hand of Raymond Poincare, former President of France, statesman, lawyer, journalist and political economist of high order. These lines denote the probability of great success and honor in public life as a result of brilliant administrative or diplomatic ability. They are known as THE LINES OF BRILLIANT DIPLOMACY.

Poincare showed rare brilliancy in early youth in his educational studies and, after serving his regulation period in the army, settled in Paris to practice law. Even a lucrative practice failed to keep him out of the politics for which he was destined. Elected to the Chamber of Deputies in his early 20s, he held that office for forty years, first as a Deputy and then as a Senator. His first public office was as Undersecretary of State, but life held greater things for him. At 33 he became Minister of Public Instruction—the youngest Minister the Third Republic has ever known. After holding various portfolios under several ministries, he was called to the premiership of France in 1912 by President Fallieres, in which capacity he distinguished himself by his far-sighted efforts to secure peace in the warring Balkans, to patch up France's differences with Germany and to consolidate France's alliance with Russia. In 1913 he was elected President of France, remaining in that office until 1920 with rare diplomacy during the troubled years of the World War. Since then he has been Prime Minister, Minister of Foreign Affairs and Minister of Finance.

Page 105

LOOK AT **YOUR** HAND

MAURICE CHEVALIER

HAVE you a sparkling personality, like Maurice Chevalier, smiling French actor? If so, you should be able to find a line commencing at the bottom of your palm, running upward and ending in a fork at the base of your third finger. This line is an asset in any one's hand. It is known as THE LINE OF PERSONALITY.

Maurice Chevalier, the brilliant and smiling idol of the screen, is in reality a very somber person. His bitter memories—a poverty-stricken childhood—war, of which he carries a constant reminder, in the form of fragments of shrapnel from German guns which are a perpetual danger to his voice, even his life.

Page 106

LOOK AT **YOUR** HAND

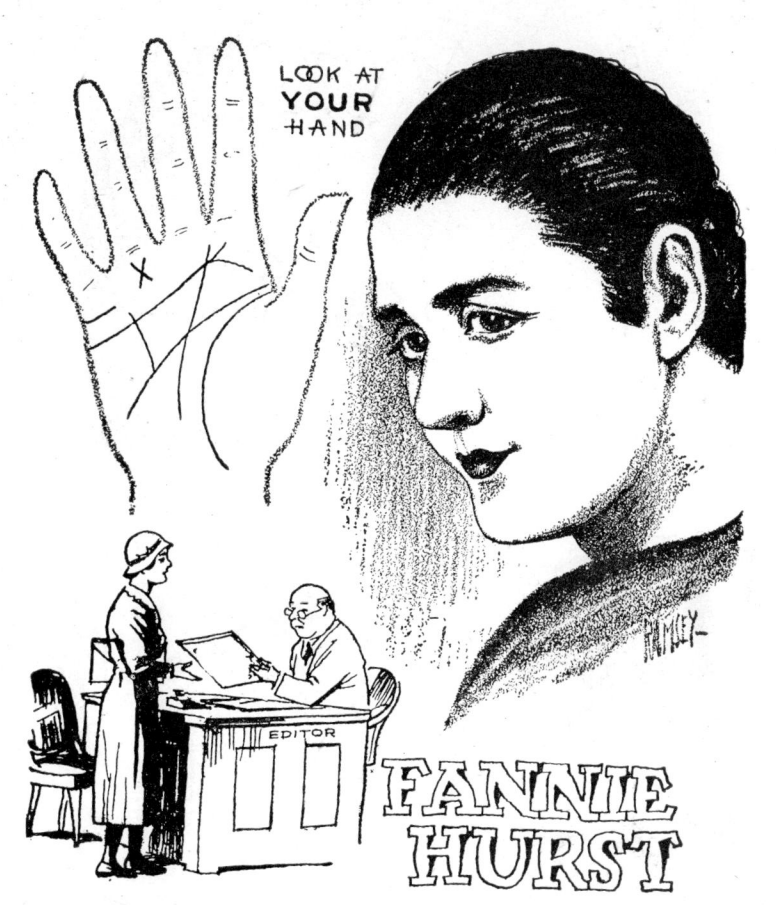

FANNIE HURST

DO YOU note all that goes on about you—and can you write about it afterward? Perhaps, like Fannie Hurst, famous author, you have a cross underneath your third finger. This cross denotes a keen sense of observation, combined with a brilliant ability to put it down on paper. It is known as THE CROSS OF KEEN OBSERVATION.

Fannie Hurst, who today is reputed to be the highest paid short-story writer in America, spent long and tedious months attempting to get editors to accept her first stories. One large magazine refused thirty-six of her stories before they finally accepted one, and only her indomitable spirit kept her from giving up her chosen work. Miss Hurst has always studied human nature. She has been interested in observing all classes of people so that she might better portray them in her works. Her activities in this line have carried her to some very unusual places. She has spent much time in New York's lower East Side, was all over Europe, and has lately made a thorough trip through Russia.

SIR HUBERT WILKINS

NORTH POLE

ARE you, like Sir Hubert Wilkins, destined to lead a life of travel and adventure? Look for a line rising from the extension of what is known as the line of life and running upward to the base of the third finger. This line denotes a life of continual travel and adventure. If you also have two little lines, one on each side of the main line, like those shown in the illustration of Sir Hubert's hand, it indicates that most of your travels will be made in the interest of scientific exploration. These lines, taken all together, are known as THE LINES OF TRAVEL AND EXPLORATION.

Sir Hubert Wilkins, the astute English explorer—a careful scientist and an intrepid commander—is possessed of the unusual gift of being able to co-ordinate science and exploration with a human interest element. It was in 1927 that he became world famous for his epic flight from Point Barrow, Alaska, to Spitzbergen. Months of preparation for this flight, discouraging obstacles and adverse weather conditions failed to faze him. After the flight was finally made, England knighted its courageous son for that feat. More recently his indomitable spirit led him to attempt to reach the North Pole by submarine, against insurmountable odds. The attempt failed, but Sir Hubert is again planning an explorative venture into the barren wastes of the frozen North.

Page 108

LOOK AT YOUR HAND

LENORE ULRIC

WILL you realize your ambitions? Look for a cross at the base of your first finger, like that clearly shown in the illustration of Lenore Ulric's hand. This sign, which insures to its owner the attainments of long-cherished ambitions, is known as THE CROSS of FULFILLED AMBITION.

The life story of Lenore Ulric reveals chapters as colorful and packed with happenings as the eventful episodes in the lives of the characters she portrays on the stage. She started her stage career in a struggling company in Milwaukee, the city of her childhood. After some years on the road her remarkable talent attracted the attention of the late David Belasco, under whose guiding hand she starred in numerous productions, perhaps the most famous being "Lulu Belle." She is considered one of the outstanding actresses on the stage today

Page 109

LOOK AT YOUR HAND

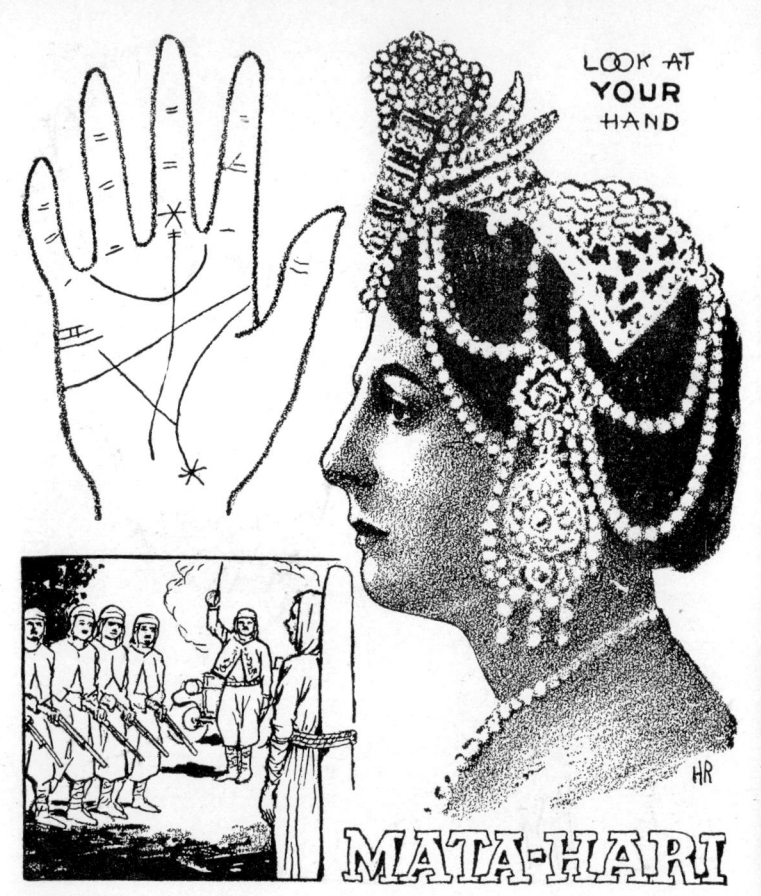

MATA-HARI

HAVE you the deadly charm of Mata Hari, the spy whose fame is world-wide, whose exploits have become a legend, and whose success in her profession is still almost inexplicable? The semicircle on the top of her palm, illustrated, denotes an active, sensual nature which, in Mata Hari's case, found outlet in her sensuous mysticism and voluptuous dancing. This semicircle is called THE GIRDLE OF VENUS.

Mata Hari's Line of Fate, seen running like a long path toward the second finger and terminating in a cross, foreshadowed her tragic and violent end. Mata Hari was destined to send men to their doom, just as her deadly charm spelled her own fate before a French firing squad. Her exploits have become a legend. Born in 1876 in Holland, she came to public attention as Mata Hari, the "Red Dancer," a glamorous Oriental dancer and courtesan. Married at 18 to an officer in the Dutch Colonial Army stationed at Java, she learned the Oriental religion and customs which were to write her into world history. Leaving her husband, she removed to Paris, where she created a sensation, not only with her sensuous interpretations of Javanese dances, but as a captivator of men. Her espionage exploits during the World War left a bloody trail of broken hearts and broken men. With satanic cunning and irresistible charm she penetrated great military secrets in the German spy service and is credited with having sent whole regiments of men to their deaths. But her beauty, glamor and notoriety were her own doom.

WALTER DAMROSCH

LOOK AT YOUR HAND

ARE you destined to become brilliant in the world of music? Perhaps, like Walter Damrosch, internationally famous conductor, you have a circle underneath your third finger. This is the sign which denotes brilliancy in music, and it is called THE CIRCLE OF MUSICAL ACCOMPLISHMENTS.

Walter Damrosch was born in Breslau, Germany, in 1862, the son of the well-known conductor and composer, Dr. Leopold Damrosch. In 1871, Dr. Damrosch came to America and was shortly afterward appointed director of the German opera. His gifted son began to attract public notice at the age of 24 by conducting Wagnerian operas. A year later he became a full-fledged conductor at the Metropolitan Opera House and of the New York Symphony Orchestra. Later he toured the entire country with his own opera company, and, in 1920, accepted the invitation of European Governments to tour Europe with the New York Symphony Orchestra. Great acclaim and signal honors were accorded him on that tour. As a special exponent of the Wagnerian school of music and as operatic conductor he proved himself a most capable leader, but his musical compositions also won him great praise. During the World War he reorganized the A. E. F. military bands and founded a school for bandmasters at the General Headquarters in France.

Page 111

LOOK AT YOUR HAND

GEORGE GERSHWIN

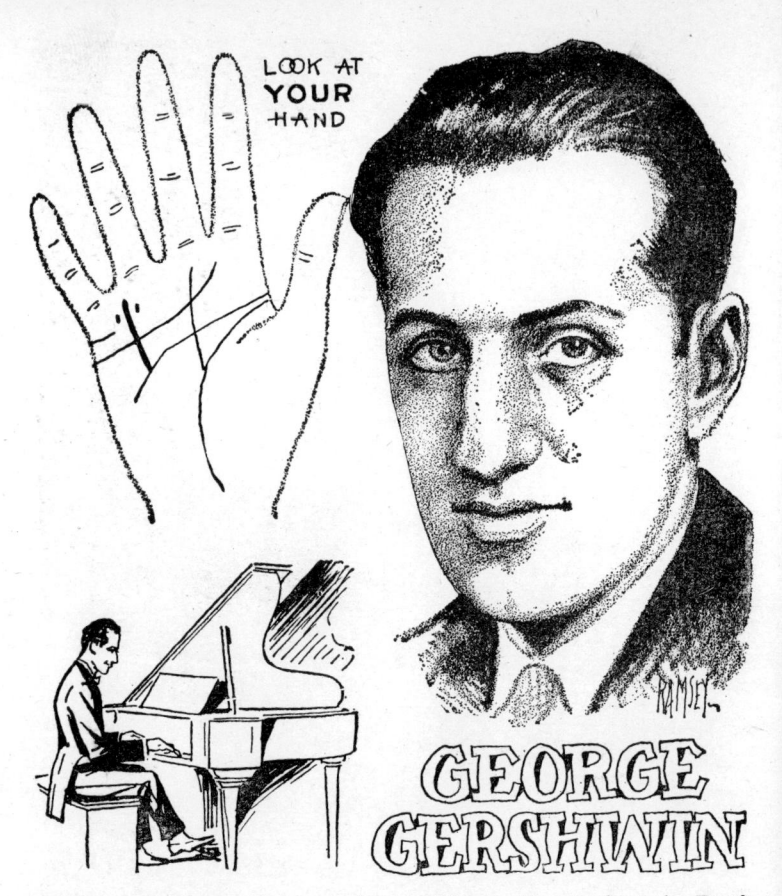

ARE you destined to become noted for your musical ability? Look for a line rising in the center of your palm, running upward, and terminating at the base between your third and fourth fingers. This line, which signifies extraordinary brilliancy and accomplishments in the art of music, is clearly shown in the illustration of George Gershwin's hand, and is known as THE LINE OF MUSICAL GENIUS.

The two little dots at each side of this line denote a rhythmic genius which manifests itself in George Gershwin's wonderful compositions. He was born in Brooklyn thirty-three years ago, took his first piano lesson when he was 13 and wrote his first song at the age of 14. He writes whenever his mood seizes him, and must be inspired. His composition, "Rhapsody in Blue," which made him world famous, was played for the first time February 12, 1924, and took him three months to write. His first really popular hit was "Swanee." He is one of the outstanding among the modern American composers.

Page 112

LOOK AT YOUR HAND

LILY PONS

WILL you win fame as the result of an exquisite voice? Perhaps, like Lily Pons, you have a circle at the base of your little finger. This is the sign of brilliant success as a result of a gifted and talented voice. It is known as THE CIRCLE OF VOCAL GENIUS.

Lily Pons, the great operatic soprano, was born in Cannes, France, of an Italian mother and a French father who also was a violinist. Perhaps the artistic temperaments of her parents brought out that talent at an earlier age than it would have manifested itself naturally. She began studying the piano at 13 in the Conservatory of Paris, and left there three years later after winning the first prize. Two years on the stage carried her in the direction of the footlights as an actress, until she heard Claudia Muzio sing "Traviata." This so inspired her that she turned to vocal training with success that brought her eventually to the Metropolitan Opera Company and great acclaim in the music world. The sweet clarity of her flute-like voice, its wide range and warmth, her expert artistry have captured the public in an age that goes on record for being "hard boiled," to prove that the sheer romance of achievement still exists.

Page 113

JACKIE COOPER

ARE you, like Jackie Cooper, a natural-born actor? Look on the side of your hand, underneath the line of head, for a small tripod. This sign, which is clearly shown in the illustration of Jackie's hand, is seen only on the palms of dramatically gifted individuals. It is known as THE TRIPOD OF BRILLIANT DRAMATIC ABILITY.

Jackie Cooper probably inherited some of the unique talent which he so brilliantly displays. His mother, Mabel Leonard, was a vaudeville violinist and his uncle, Norman Taurog, is a well-known movie director. Jack was born in Los Angeles on September 15, 1923, and already as a tot played small parts in comedies, which netted him $5 a day. He makes a good deal more now, being reputedly the highest paid child star on the screen today. He is a modest and most likable youngster with blond hair and sparkling hazel eyes.

Page 114

LOOK AT **YOUR** HAND

ELISSA LANDI

Have you a tremendous imagination? Perhaps, like Elissa Landi, who is noted equally for her beauty, her dramatic ability and her writing ability, you have a circle on the side of your palm. This sign, which is clearly shown in the illustration of Elissa Landi's hand denotes a vividly creative imagination. It is known as THE CIRCLE OF VIVID IMAGINATION.

Elissa Landi, besides being a brilliant actress, is also a novelist, having written a number of novels. She was born in Venice, Italy, daughter of the Countess Zanardi-Landi, of the Austrian nobility. She started her career on the stage in an English repertory company in Oxford in order to secure material to write plays, but her talent soon attracted the attention of the motion-picture producers, who brought her to Hollywood under contract. She scored heavily in her first picture, and her brilliant portrayals since then have earned her a secure place among the most talented stars.

Page 115

RUDYARD KIPLING

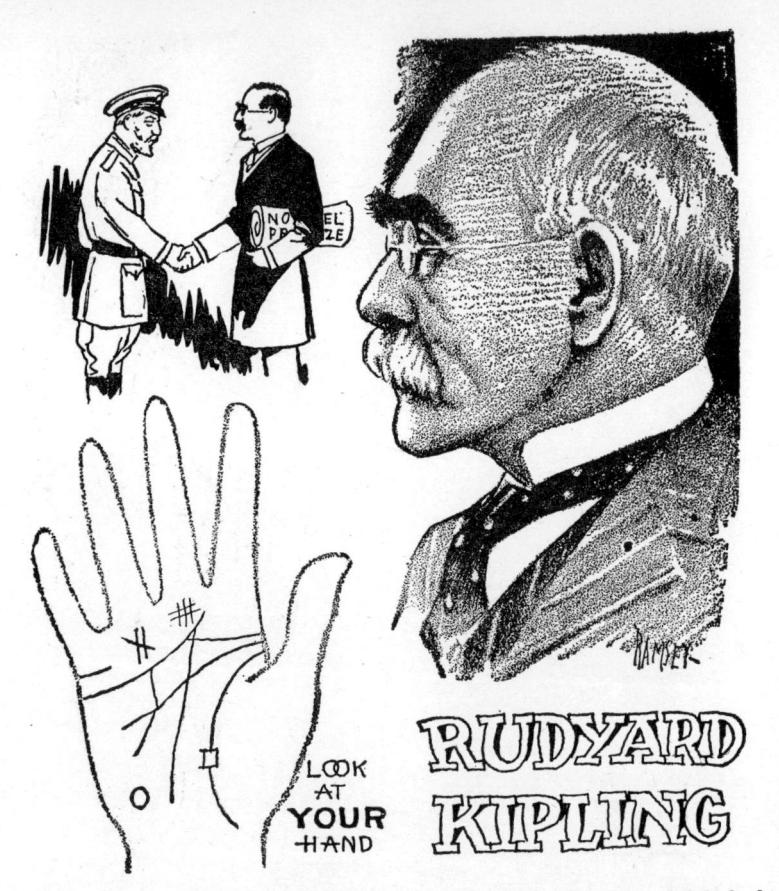

DID Fate destine you to become a poet? Look for three lines crossing each other underneath your third finger, like those clearly shown in the illustration of Kipling's hand. These lines, often seen on the hands of gifted poets, are known as THE LINES OF POETIC GENIUS.

The glamour, color and magic of Rudyard Kipling, great English patriot and poet, also mark his literary works which have influenced thought almost without precedent. Born in Bombay, India, in 1865, he spent his early years in Lahore, where his father was curator of the museum. But it was in England, where he pursued his later education, that he first learned the art of story-telling in the dormitories, when classmates listened avidly to the tales he spun both from memory and from imagination. Returned to India, he went into newspaper work. As sub-editor for the Allahabad Pioneer, he started writing the verses and stories which were to make him famous. His first published book of verse, "Departmental Ditties," at the age of 21, was an instant success. Subsequently, his books were each a literary event, for they are crowded with an individual charm. Although he has been hailed as the greatest English poet since Tennyson, Kipling's official recognition, in the appointment of Poet Laureate, was thwarted by politics for his own written views. But in 1906 he was awarded the Nobel Prize. Of recent years his output has dwindled almost to the point of complete retirement. But he has become a legendary figure in English and world literature, this "Man From Nowhere."

Page 116

LOOK AT **YOUR HAND**

BABE RUTH

HAVE you the power of mind over muscle that makes a great sportsman? Look for an upward curve, extending from the end of what is known as the Line of Head (which begins under the first finger and runs straight across the palm.) This curve, which denotes a power of concentration and perfect co-ordination of mind and muscle, is clearly shown in the illustration of Babe Ruth's hand. It is known as THE LINE OF MENTAL AND MUSCULAR CO-ORDINATION.

Babe Ruth is no doubt one of the greatest "natural" ball players on record. Born of humble parents in Baltimore, he rose through his own efforts to fame and fortune without letting his success turn his head. For many years the home run king has been outstanding in baseball.

Page 117

MAXIM GORKY

IS YOUR life difficult and full of hardship? Perhaps, like Maxim Gorky, famous Russian writer, you have a cross on your hand underneath the second finger—but perhaps, like him, you will find compensation in popular acclaim. This cross, denoting a life full of hardship and suffering, is known as THE CROSS OF BITTERNESS.

This famous Russian writer, born in 1868 on the shores of the Volga, assumed the name Maxim Gorky, meaning "Maxim, the Bitter," when he began his literary career at the age of 24 with the publication of "Mokar Tschundra." To the hardship and suffering of his bitter childhood experiences—misery, destitution and hopelessness—he has left his name as a monument in the literary world. Orphaned at 9 and homeless, he wandered aimlessly among fellow unfortunates, gathering the bitterness and despair which mark his works. During his vagabondage he learned to read and write and began to write of his sufferance and the misery he witnessed in the lowest stratum of humanity. An unhappy destiny, indeed, but one which has established him as the national folk writer of Russia, acclaimed successor to Chekhov, Tolstoy and Dostoievsky. Banished by the Imperial Government, he visited America in 1906 and later settled on the Island of Capri, where he lived in the hope that the climate would heal his tubercular lungs. Back in Russia after the downfall of the Czarist regime, he fought in the World War and later became reconciled to Bolshevism. But his inherent bitterness has remained unswerved.

Page 118

LOOK AT **YOUR** HAND

GENE TUNNEY

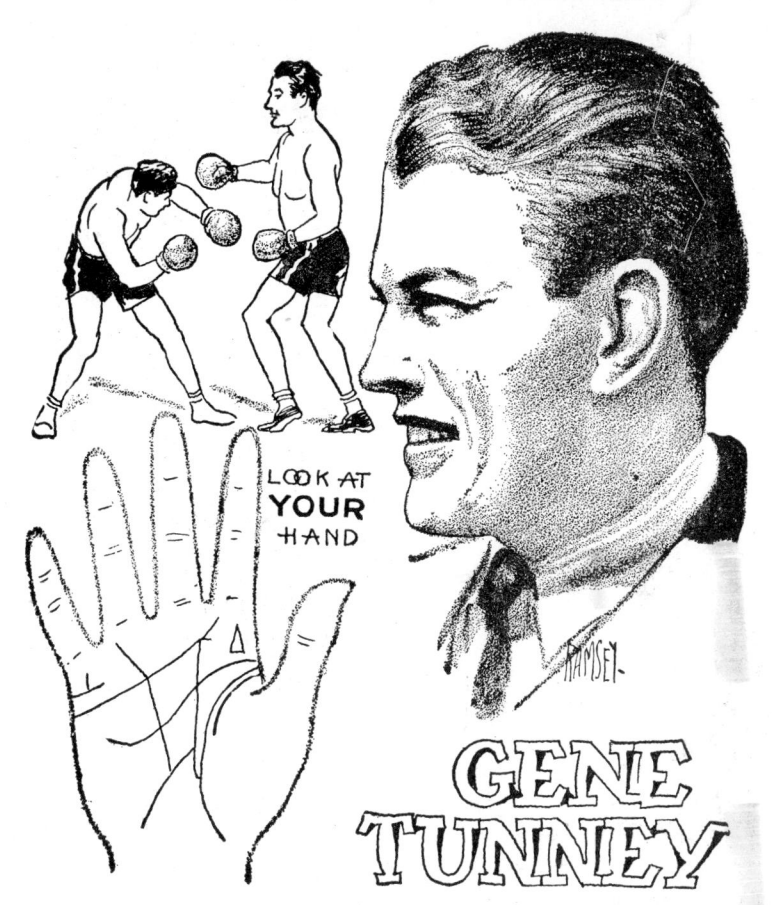

HAVE you what is sometimes called the greatest of all blessings—perfect health? Look for a line inside the line of life, opposite the thumb, like that clearly shown in Gene Tunney's palm, illustrated above. This sign denotes the possession of perfect health and great vitality. It is known as THE LINE OF VITALITY.

Throughout his career, which finds him now in the prime of life, this gentleman pugilist forged ahead to the peak of fistic fame as world's heavyweight champion. Born in New York in 1898, he became a shipping clerk, a position which he held until America's entrance into the World War. It was in the service in the Marine Corps in France that he became interested in boxing. Gradually, steadily, he fought his way to the light-heavyweight championship of the American Expeditionary Forces. Demobilized, he entered the professional ranks and won victories over Georges Carpentier, Ermino Spalla and Tommy Gibbons, which made him challenger of Jack Dempsey's title. His defeat of Dempsey in Philadelphia in 1926 was sensational, as was the famous return bout in Chicago, from which he emerged victor. But Tunney had no illusions about the prize ring. It was an "Open Sesame" to him to quick wealth. But he turned his rather ordinary physique into one of the finest pieces of ring machinery of all time. His will power and self-discipline opened the doors to the fortune he sought, and which has enabled him since retiring from the ring, to cultivate his hobbies of books, art and music. His intimates are men of learning and achievement.

Page 119

LOOK AT YOUR HAND

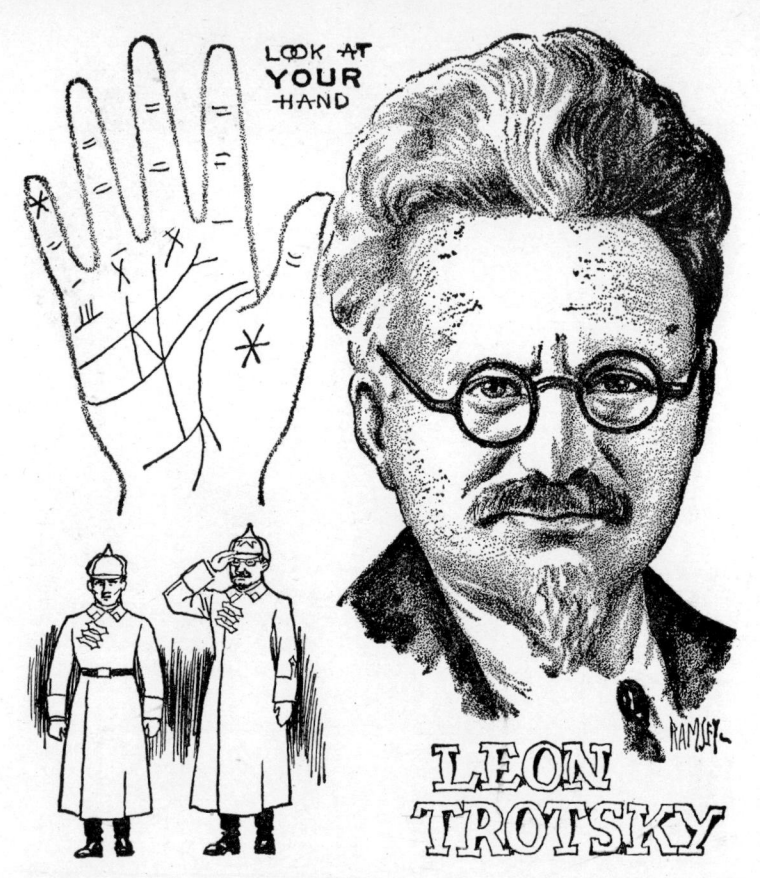

LEON TROTSKY

ARE you destined to become noted for the persuasive power of your speech? Look for a star on the tip of your fourth finger, like that clearly shown in the illustration of the hand of Leon Trotsky, first Minister of War of the Soviet Republic. This sign denotes a power of eloquence that by the passion of its conviction is able to sway an audience. It is known as THE STAR OF ELOQUENCE

Trotsky, who was one of the founders of the Communist Government in Russia and, at one time, perhaps the strongest figure in the Soviet regime, was born in 1879 to become at 17 leader of a revolutionary organization. Exiled to Siberia for his activities, he escaped, obtaining a false passport to which he signed the name which has written him into history as one of the two most famous men to come out of the new Russia, Lenin being the other. His wanderings in exile took him to Austria, Switzerland, Paris, London and America, where he wrote and lectured on the principles of Karl Marx. At the outbreak of the Russian Revolution of 1917, he became Minister of War of the new Soviet Republic and exerted great power and discipline. His powers were weakened by Lenin's death. He was ousted from office, and, in 1924, was denounced by the Communist Party for his literary activities, being accused of heresy. He lost the control of the Government to Stalin, and resumed his career of exile. His influence has all but vanished, but the name of Trotsky will live on in world history.

KATE SMITH

ARE you, like Kate Smith, destined to become famous as a result of a lyric quality in your own nature? Look for a line running from the base of the second finger toward the fourth, like that clearly shown in this famous radio singer's hand. This sign denotes brilliancy in lyrical expression, and is known as THE LINE OF LYRICAL EXPRESSION.

In Kate Smith, this lyric quality maniests itself in her beautiful singing. Almost overnight she became the favorite of millions of people in this country as a result of her radio performance. Her voice carries such emotional appeal that it grips the hearts of her listeners. By nature of a very jolly disposition, she brings with her singing cheer into many homes.

Page 121

LOOK AT YOUR HAND

SIR OLIVER LODGE

ARE you a mystic? Perhaps, like Sir Oliver Lodge, scientist and spiritualist, you have a cross in the center of your palm between the lines of head and heart. This sign, denoting a natural inclination toward mysticism and occultism of all kinds, is clearly shown in Sir Oliver's hand, and is called THE MYSTIC CROSS.

This great scientist, whose work in physics is unsurpassed in modern times, was born in 1851 in England. His unusual scientific talents showed themselves in him at an early age. At 6 he was fascinated by the whys and wherefores of the mechanism of engines. Overcoming his father's disapproval of his leanings, he studied hard to cultivate his inborn inclinations. A pioneer in wireless communication, he developed and improved various theories which made wireless telegraphy possible long before the days of Marconi. As a result of his researches in wireless and electroc-magnetic waves, he was made a Fellow in the Royal Society in 1900, and, later. was knighted by King Edward. The higher aspects of religion then drew his interest as he tried to reconcile them with scientific doctrines. In 1908 he first startled the world with his belief in communication with the dead—a theory by which he is probably best known to the lay public. The death of his son, Raymond, in the war was followed by a remrakable book, "Raymond," which purported to be an account of messages received from his dead son. This book was widely read, and created much discussion.

Page 122

LOOK AT YOUR HAND

WM. T. TILDEN 2nd.

ARE you destined to become as noted a sportsman as Big Bill Tilden, of tennis fame? Look for a triangle underneath your first finger, like that clearly shown in the illustration of Tilden's hand. This sign denotes superior sportsmanship, combined, in his case, with brilliant dramatic abilty. It is known as THE LINE OF SUPERIOR SPORTSMANSHIP.

William T. Tilden's innate sense of the dramatic never fails to affect his audiences. His mastery of tennis does not extend merely to production of its strokes or to the most thorough analysis of the uses and effects of spin that has probably ever been made, but he knows the game inside and out, its rules and regulations and everything else. There is no doubt that tennis, since its origin, never had a greater, more picturesque or popular champion.

Page 123

LOOK AT YOUR HAND

JANET GAYNOR

DID Fate endow you with charm? Look for a tripod at the top of your palm between the third and fourth fingers, like that clearly shown in the illustration of Janet Gaynor's hand. If you find it, you have a charming, somewhat shy, nature. This sign is known as THE TRIPOD OF CHARM.

Janet Gaynor, brilliant and popular screen star, was born in Philadelphia. Her first name is Laura. After her graduation from high school her parents moved to San Francisco, and there she worked first as a cashier in a store and then as an usheress in a theatre. Her first movie work was as an extra and later she played bits in slapstick comedies. Her first important role was in a picture known as "The Johnstown Flood," but it was the picture "Seventh Heaven" which brought her fame and won her rating as a star.

LOOK AT YOUR HAND

Mrs. AIMEE McPHERSON

IS YOUR nature made up of contradictions? Look in your hand: If you have a triangle in the center of your palm, underneath your middle finger, you have so many contradictory qualities that you may be either sinner or saint, and only the modification of all the lines can throw light as to your characteristics and destiny. This sign is known as THE TRIANGLE OF CONTRADICTORY CHARACTERISTICS.

Born in rural Ontario, Canada, the daughter of a farmer and a woman who had been a Salvation Army lassie, Sister Aimee Semple McPherson showed early an interest in amateur theatricals and became herself quite an amateur actress. She was converted at 17 by Robert Semple, a handsome young Scotch evangelist, whom she married and with whom she went as a missionary to China. At the Rev. Mr. Semple's death, she returned home and married Harold McPherson, a well-to-do grocer who, on her refusal to quit preaching, divorced her, and she became a traveling evangelist. After some years on the road she finally settled in Los Angeles and there built the Four Square Gospel Angelus Temple, of which she is head. By her own description she is "God's star saleswoman."

Page 125

LOOK AT **YOUR** HAND

GRAND-DUCHESS ANASTASIA

IS YOUR life destined to be shrouded in mystery? Look for "islands" at the commencement and termination of the line of Destiny (which runs lengthwise through the center of the palm). These islands indicate that some great mystery affects the life of the individual. They are known as THE ISLANDS OF MYSTERY.

Madame Tchaikowsky, who calls herself the Grand Duchess Anastasia and who claims to be the only surviving child of the ex-Czar Nicholas of Russia, has created a sensation in the royal courts of Europe. While many claim that she is an impostor, others very near to the late imperial family of Russia, state that they really recognize in her the daughter of the late Czar. This writer, who has in his possession an original imprint of the right hand of Czar Nicholas II, in comparing it with the palm of Madame Tchaikowsky, found such an amazing hereditary similarity of the two palms that he has no doubt of the truthfulness of her claim. By what miracle she has escaped death this writer cannot say, however, the similarity of these two palms, of which no other two in the world are alike, is so striking that the fact of her genuineness seems self-evident.

Page 126

MAE WEST

LOOK AT YOUR HAND

HAVE you a vivid, but perhaps somewhat sensual, imagination? If you find a semicircle at the top of your palm, running between the first and the fourth fingers, you probably have. This semicircle is known as THE GIRDLE OF VENUS.

Mae West, actress and playright, known for her daring themes and acting, started her theatrical career by doing imitations of Eddie Foy and Bert Williams. Her first big role was in "Sometime." Later she appeared in various reviews, finally starring in her own plays, some of them bringing her notoriety, others fame.

Page 127

LOOK AT YOUR HAND

MARIE DRESSLER

WILL you attain your ambitions like Marie Dressler, beloved actress? Look for a cross underneath your first finger, for this sign insures to its owner the attainment of long-cherished ambitions. It is called THE CROSS OF FULFILLED AMBITIONS.

Marie Dressler, famous stage and screen star, made her first public appearance at the age of 5, at a church theatrical performance. Since then, she has played every possible part on the stage, from the chorus up, was with Weber and Fields in the old music hall, New York, and was later featured in opera and comedy. She started years ago in slapstick comedies, like "Tillie's Punctured Romance," and later switched to more serious parts. In 1931 she received the gold medal from the Academy of Motion Pictures for the outstanding performance as an actress of the year. Her real name is Leila Koerber. She adopted her present name from an aunt.

Page 128

ALLA NAZIMOVA

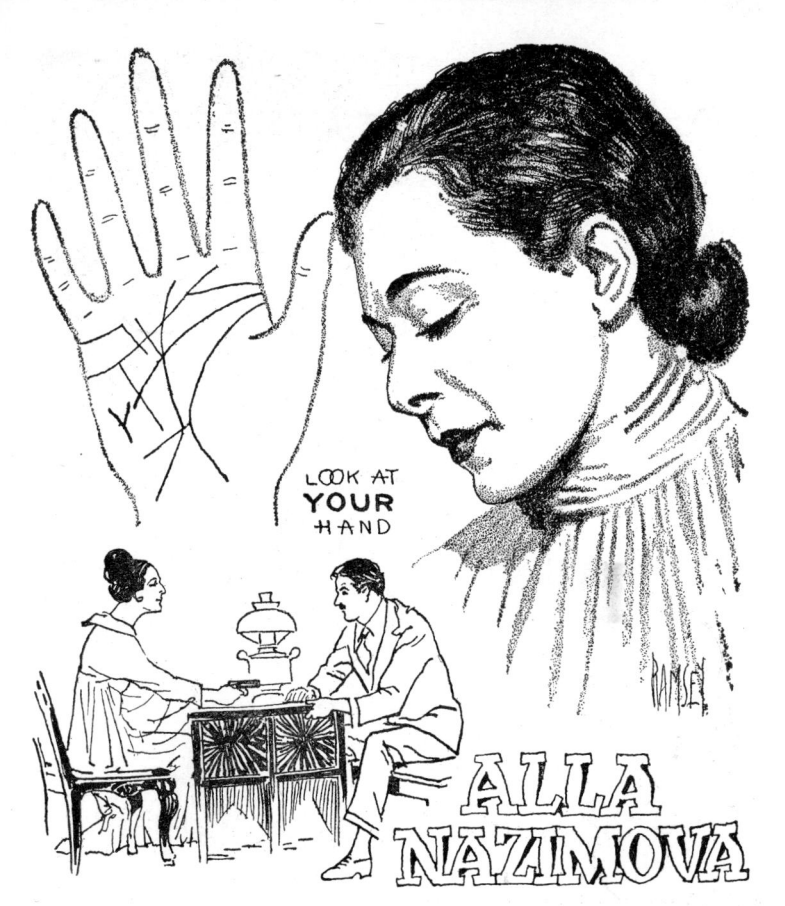

LOOK AT YOUR HAND

WERE you born with a talent for acting? Look in your hand: if you see a tripod at the bottom of your palm, toward the side, you have natural talent in dramatic expression. This sign, clearly shown in the illustration of Nazimova's hand, is known as THE TRIPOD OF DRAMATIC EXPRESSION.

Alla Nazimova, world famous actress, was born in Yalta, Russia, of poor but educated Jewish parents who were radicals and were forced to flee for their lives from massacres and outrages. She started her stage career at the age of 23, first playing on the Jewish stage, and then became one of the best known and loved actresses on the screen. At present she is considered one of the outstanding dramatic actresses on the stage

Page 129

LOOK AT **YOUR** HAND

NORMA SHEARER

DID a kind fate endow you with natural charm? If you, like Norma Shearer, famous actress, have a tripod on your palm, underneath your third finger, you have a charming, unconventional nature and a love of entertaining. You make a perfect host or hostess. This sign is known as **THE TRIPOD OF CHARM**.

Norma Shearer was born in Westmount, a suburb of Montreal, Canada. She came to New York in 1920, trying to break into the movies and almost failed in the first attempt. Her first important part that attracted attention was in the "Student Prince." It was, however, the talkies that really brought out her talent, and her performance in the "Trial of Mary Dugan," and "The Divorcee," was considered outstanding. In 1929 she was given the award of the Academy of Motion Picture Arts and Sciences, for the best performance by a screen actress of that year. Besides being known as one of the best-dressed women on the screen, she has an astute business head, and is considered a very brilliant conversationalist. She has been married for a number of years to Irving G. Thalberg.

LOOK AT YOUR HAND

BERTRAND RUSSELL

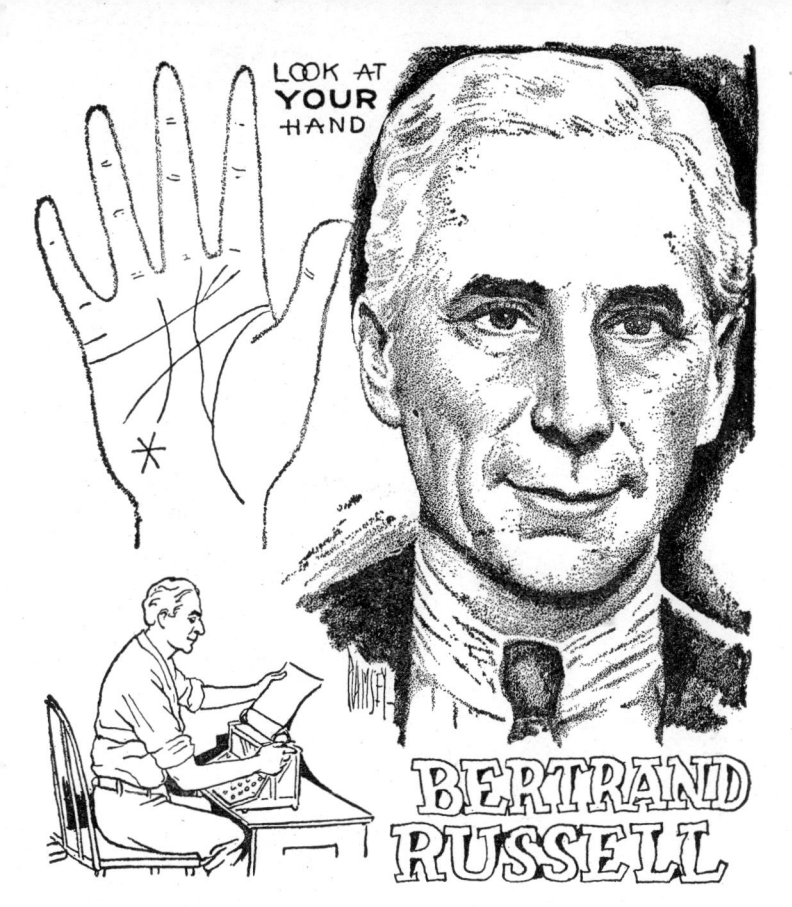

ARE you destined to become noted for your intelligence? Perhaps, like Bertrand Russell, you have a star on the bottom of your palm, in line with the third finger. This sign denotes great honors to its possessor as the result of a brilliant and versatile mind. It is known as THE STAR OF BRILLIANT INTELLECT.

Born in Trelleck, England, in 1872, and educated at Trinity College, Cambridge, Bertrand Russell later became lecturer and fellow of the same college.

His world-wide travels, liberal opinions and philosophical and mathematical writings have since given him international repute. For many years he has been the storm center of intellectual controversies because of his unorthodox and frequently radical opinions on education, marriage and other social problems. Soon after the outbreak of the World War, he attracted attention with his activities in behalf of the nonconscription fellowship and was fined for writing a leaflet, "Unconscieutious Objections." In 1918 he was condemned for his pacifist views to six months' imprisonment. In 1920, after a visit to Russia, articles written by him on Sovietism drew wide attention. Despite all this, his fame as a moral pholosopher remains undisputed.

Page 131

LOOK AT YOUR HAND

ARTURO TOSCANINI

HAVE you the temperament of an artist? Perhaps, like Arturo Toscanini, famed for many years as conductor at the Metropolitan Opera House and equally celebrated as leader of symphonic orchestras, you have a line extending from what is known as the line of heart, running toward the side of the hand under the first finger. This line denotes a lively temperament generally coupled with strong artistic tendencies. It is known as THE LINE OF ARTISTIC TEMPERAMENT.

Toscanini's rare musical talent evidenced itself at an early age. Born in Parma, Italy, in 1867, he became a pupil at the Milan Conservatory. Completing his studies, he joined the Scala Orchestra as a 'cellist. Happenstance turned his career at his point, when the regular conductor fell ill. Toscanini volunteered to conduct, and did so, from memory, with such brilliancy that he was induced to exchange the bow for the conductor's baton. Since then his success in the music world has made him probably the greatest living conductor. To him artistic integrity is paramount. He has no tolerance for anything but the highest in his art. He is both loved and feared by his musicians. His temperament is one of those extremely effective ones which are immediately translated into action, and his acts are instantaneous releases which overwhelm players and audiences alike by their outbursts. He is a man of great simplicity and warm-heartedness in private life, but inflexible in everything pertaining to his art. But this very temperament has given him world-wide recognition, his mastery unquestioned, as he has moved and thrilled countless thousands. From 1908 to 1921 he was conductor at the Metropolitan Opera House in New York, a most coveted prize.

Page 132

LOOK AT YOUR HAND

SIR RABINDRANATH TAGORE

HAVE you the sixth sense called intuition? Look for a line on the side of your hand, beginning under the fourth finger and running in the form of a semicircle down the palm. This line, clearly shown in the hand of Sir Rabindranath Tagore, Hindu philosopher and poet, signifies intuitive inspiration manifesting itself in many ways, in the arts, philosophy, poetry, social justice and in other fields. It is known as THE LINE OF INTUITIVE WISDOM.

Tagore's career has served to link the Orient with the Occident. It has made him the best-known emissary of Eastern thought and culture, with the possible exception of Gandhi. Born in India in 1861, of a family of sages revered throughout India, he went to England at 16 to study law. Returning to India, he began writing, pursuing his one ideal—that all people of the earth should live in harmony, each having his own place in the sun and each contributing to the welfare of the whole. At the institution Visva-Bharati, which he founded in Bengal in 1901, he tried to further education and to abolish all class and religious distinction. His writings and poetry have by now been translated into almost every civilized language. In 1933 he was awarded the Nobel Prize for Literature—the first exponent of the Orient to receive that recognition. The English Government knighted him in 1915, and the world paid him homage in his extensive travels in Europe, South America, the United States and the Far East.

LOOK AT YOUR HAND

MRS. CALVIN COOLIDGE

WHEN people speak of you, do they always use the word "charming"? The lines denoting a naturally charming personality are found at the top of the palm, terminating underneath the first finger. This sign, clearly shown in Mrs. Coolidge's hand, is known as THE LINES OF NATURAL CHARM.

Of all the "First Ladies of the Land" within recent memory, none won broader esteem and admiration than Grace Coolidge. Her charm radiated from the portals of the White House, where she was mistress for six years. Born in Burlington, Vt., she went to public school, high school and on to the University of Vermont. Through a friend Mrs. Coolidge became interested in teaching the deaf and, prior to her marriage, taught in the Clarke School for the Deaf at Northampton, Mass. Later she became the bride of Calvin Coolidge, then a young, serious-minded, hard-working lawyer, and their first home was a little double house where two boys were born to them, John and Calvin. Calvin died July 7, 1924, while the President was in office, and the whole Nation mourned with the "First Family." As wife and mother of her young family, as First Lady of the great Commonwealth of Massachusetts during her husband's term as Governor of that State, and as counselor and adviser of the Nation's Chief Executive, she displayed a poise, graciousness, gentility, high intelligence and a human understanding that have placed her high in the ranks of America's most charming women.

LOOK AT YOUR HAND

PEGGY JOYCE

"WELL, PEGGY, HOW MANY DO YOU WANT TO-DAY?"

AT WHAT age will you marry? How many times? Will you be happy or unhappy in your marriage? The answer to these questions lies on the side of the hand at the base of the fourth finger. The number of parallel lines cutting across the edge of the hand, above the end of the heart line, tells the number of marriages you will make. Only the deep and clearly formed lines relate to marriage; the short ones pertain to deep affections. If a line is found close to the line of heart it indicates marriage at an early age. If found in the middle between the line of heart and the base of the little finger, it denotes marriage at the age of about 25 or 30. If found close to the base of the fourth finger, it signifies a marriage rather late in life.

Peggy Hopkins Joyce is known for her many matrimonial ventures, which are clearly indicated in the above illustration of her hand.

Page 135

LOOK AT **YOUR** HAND

SIGMUND FREUD

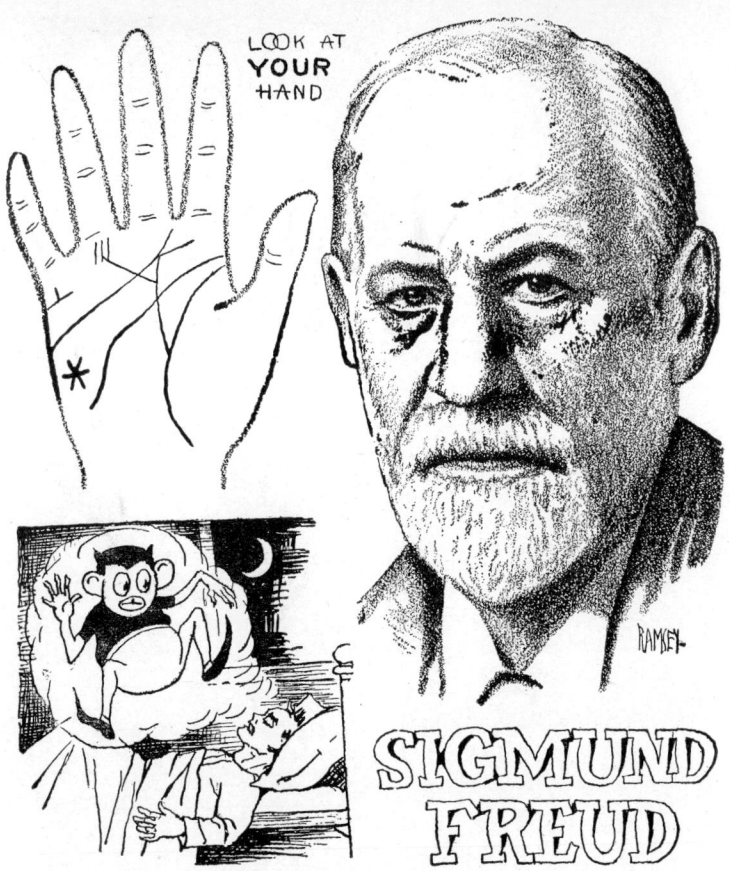

ARE you destined to become noted for your brilliant reasoning powers? Look for a star in the center of your palm under your fourth finger, since this is a sign of great ability and probable fame in the realm of science and philosophy. It is known as THE STAR OF BRILLIANT REASONING.

The celebrated scientist, Sigmund Freud, who is accredited with the foundation of psycho-analysis, was born of Jewish parents in Moravia in 1856. Influenced by Gothe's "Die Natur," he studied medicine. But his gifted reasoning powers destined him for immortal fame in a wider field—psychology. It was an experience, extraordinary then, in which symptoms of hysteria were cured by inducing the patient, under hypnosis, to recall the circumstances of its origin and to express the accompanying emotions, that started Freud on psycho-analysis. Revolutionizing the treatment of neurotic disorders from the psychological aspect, he established a new school of thought which has left an indelible stamp. His discoveries of mental abnormalities, such as delusions, dreams, etc., as representations of fulfillment of suppressed desires, have explained an age-old mystery. To the general public, it is probably less the application of psycho-analysis to the abnormal than to the normal mental phenomena which is of greatest interest, for it has enabled man to know himself better, though it may not have made him happier.

Page 136

ANDREW W. MELLON

RICH man, poor man, which will you be? If you are destined to become wealthy, you may find a star at the base of your third finger, denoting success in business and finance. In fact, the proverbial luck of those whose hands bear this mark is so remarkable that almost anything they touch turns to gold. This sign is known as THE STAR OF FORTUNE.

Statistics speak for the truth of this sign in the case of Andrew Mellon, son of an Irish immigrant whose business acumen and knowledge of finance have established one of the greatest fortunes in America and three times made him Secretary of the United States Treasury. Born in Pittsburgh, Pa., in 1855, Andrew Mellon first became a Judge, then banker and business man. At 25 he became head of T. Mellon & Sons, the bank which was the forerunner of the wide interests controlled by the Mellons today. Coal, railroads, oil and aluminum then joined to build their great holdings. When Andrew Mellon resigned from private business to become Secretary of the Treasury in 1921, he was holding office as director or officer in 160 corporations. His reduction of taxes and public debt during his Secretaryship were outstanding achievements. On his resignation from the Cabinet he was designated Ambassador to England in 1932. He is quiet and reserved, with a love of art, work and his two children.

Page 137

LOOK AT YOUR HAND

DR. ROY CHAPMAN ANDREWS

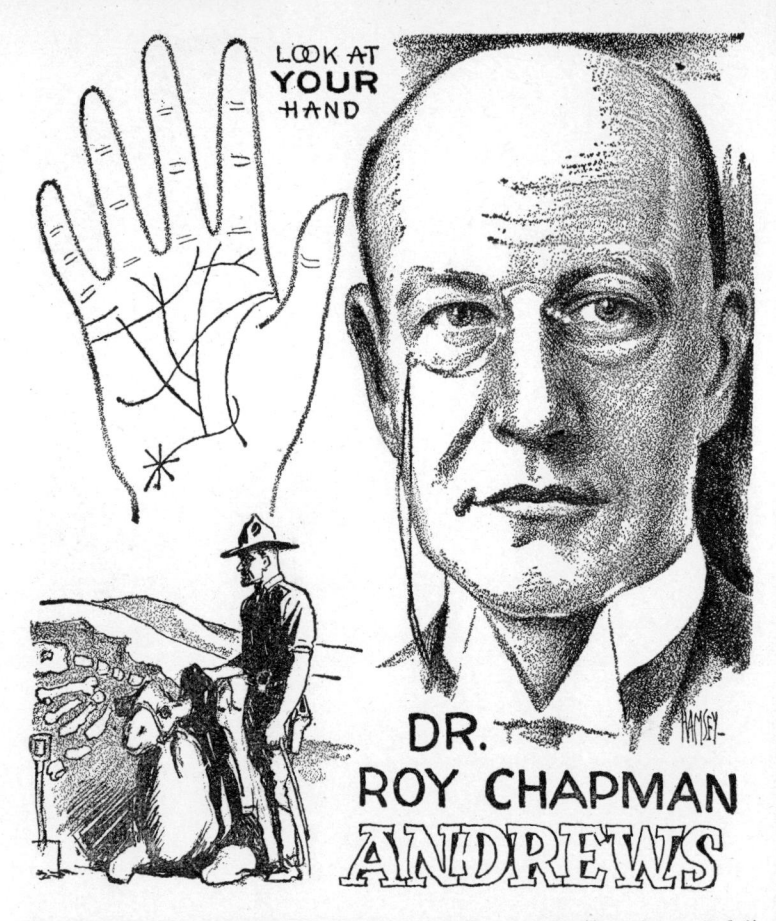

IS THE star of travel in your hand? It is found on the side of the hand on a branch running from what is known as the line of life (which circles the thumb). Clearly shown in the illustration of Dr. Roy Chapman Andrews' hand, it denotes a life of continual travel and adventure in the interest of scientific exploration. It is called THE STAR OF TRAVEL AND EXPLORATION.

Roy Chapman Andrews, the famous explorer, was born on January 26, 1884, in the town of Beloit, Wis., and after graduating from Beloit College he became connected with the American Museum of Natural History in New York, and since then has led many expeditions in different parts of the world, enriching science with his discoveries. His most spectacular one was his expedition to Central Asia, where, while hunting prehistoric fossils, he discovered and after many hardships and hair-raising adventures brought back the now famous dragon eggs.

Page 138

DINO GRANDI

LOOK AT YOUR HAND

HAVE you the ability to become a great statesman? Look at your hand. If you find three lines extending from what is known as the line of head, like those in the illustrated hand of Dino Grandi, noted Italian diplomat, you have diplomatic genius. These are known as THE LINES OF BRILLIANT DIPLOMATIC ABILITY.

Signor Dino Grandi, Italy's enthusiastic and readily likable Foreign Minister, was born at Mordano, a village near Bologna, June 4, 1895. After attending the Lyceum at Bologna at 19 he had just entered the law school when Italy joined the Allies in the World War. He enlisted as a private in the Alpine Infantry, being made within a year a second lieutenant and becoming a captain at the age of 22. He fought with great valor and earned various medals. He was one of the leaders of the march of the Fascisti on Rome, and it was he who conducted the negotiations with King Victor Emanuel. In 1929 Mussolini gave up seven of the nine portfolios which he held in the Fascist Government, and Grandi, at the age of 34, became Minister of Foreign Affairs. Grandi, once a man of arms, a fiery orator and writer, is now a persuasive but still dynamic negotiator who captures the fancy of the public with his compelling personality.

Page 139

LOOK AT YOUR HAND

GEN. JAN C. SMUTS

CAN you do a great many things well? Perhaps, like General Jan Christian Smuts, you have the lines at the end of your line of head (which runs across the palm below the heart line) which indicate capacity for brilliant achievements in many branches of activity. They are known as THE LINES OF BRILLIANT VERSATILITY.

General Smuts, born in 1870, has distinguished himself as soldier, statesman, lawyer, philosopher and botanist, and has held many high offices. His energy and love of resolute action have carried him through many storms in his career. In the Boer War he fought against Great Britain with "Oom" Kruger and became famous as one of the ablest generals of the Boer Army.

After the defeat of the cause of the Boer Republics by the overwhelming power of the British Empire, he made his peace with the victor, and entered the service of the new order under British rule. In the World War he led Boers and Britishers against the Germans in East Africa. After the war he took a prominent part in the peace treaty, and the establishment of the League of Nations as author of the Mandate system, and has remained one of the leaders of the South African Party.

These lines are very often seen in the hands of prominent diplomats and lawyers. Here I want to stress the fact that, since there are no two hands alike, one line means a certain quality, and it is the combination of all lines which determines the character or destiny of an individual.

LOOK AT YOUR HAND

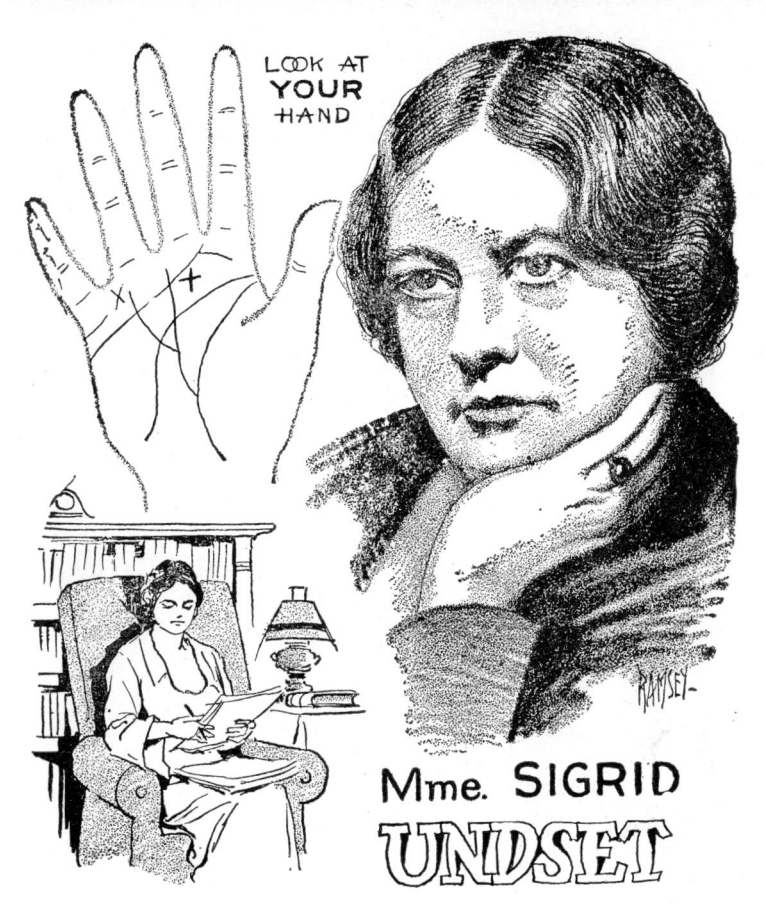

Mme. SIGRID UNDSET

HAVE you, like Sigrid Undset, celebrated Danish novelist, the CROSS OF RELIGIOUS INSPIRATION in your hand? Look for it in the center of your palm under your second finger. This sign, clearly shown in this great writer's hand, denotes a nature inclined toward religious mysticism.

Sigrid Undset gained fame chiefly through her ability to depict feminine character. This aspect of her work is evident even in her first stories, "The Happy Age" and "Martha Oulie." Her early life gave no hint of the great honors which were to be hers. Born May 20, 1882, at Kallundborg, Denmark, her father was Ingwald Undset, Norwegian archeologist, who was director of the National Museum at Oslo. The father died early, leaving his family in poverty, and from 1899 to 1909, the author earned her living by working as a clerk. Her first novel, "Jenny," was published in 1911, followed by several volumes of children's stories, but it is chiefly through her historical novel "Kristin Lovrensdatter" that she became world famous.

Page 141

LOOK AT YOUR HAND

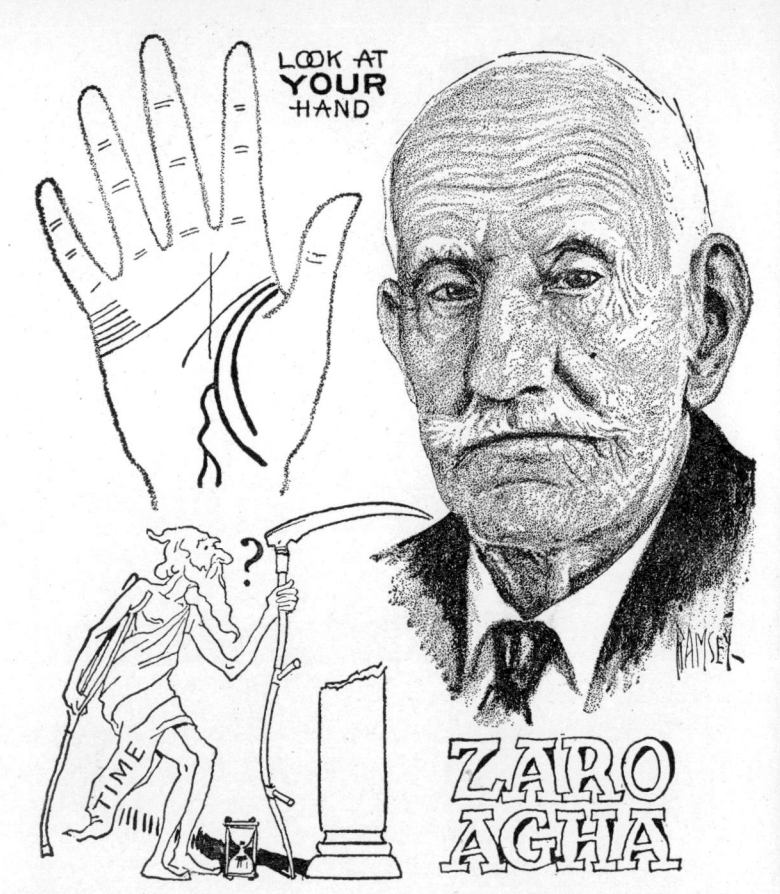

ZARO AGHA

How long will you live? Who isn't interested in a personal answer to that question! If you are destined to live far longer than the average man or woman, you will find two lines running around the base of your thumb. The first line is your life line. The inner line, known as the double line of life, strengthens the first, so that together they denote an exceptionally long life, vitality, freedom from illness and strength of constitution. They are known as THE LINES OF METHUSELAH.

Truly, this modern age has seen no parallel to the aged Turk, Zaro Agha, who claims to be 158 years of age. America got a glimpse of him a few years ago and marveled at his agility, sense of humor and more than seven score years. Those years have been fruitful years, for twelve marriages bore thirty-six children. However, all of his progeny are now dead, with the exception of one daughter, who was born when Agha was 96. The years have been too many for him to keep track of his other descendants. For 112 years he worked as a porter, his last job being that of piano mover in a factory. Between times he went to war and served in no less than fourteen campaigns. Agha claims that he has never tasted alcoholic beverages in the entire span of his long life and that tobacco is unknown to him. He subsists mainly on vegetables and sweets, and humorously avers that the first hundred years were the easiest.

Page 142

JEDDU KRISHNAMURTI

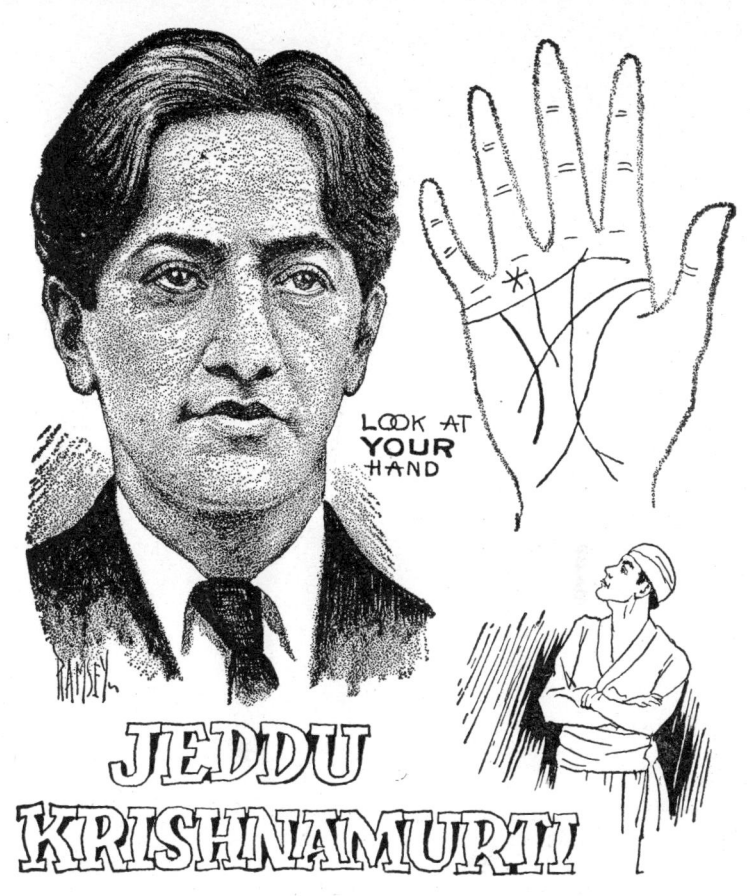

ARE you naturally intuitive? Perhaps, like Jeddu Krishnamurti, Brahmin messiah of the Theosophists, you have a line commencing on the side of your hand, under the fourth finger, and running in a semicircle down the palm. This line indicates a very highly strung and sensitive person, with an acute sense of intuition that manifests itself in feelings of presentiment, and strange, vivid dreams which, very remarkably, often come true, a phenomenon few people are able to explain. In most of such cases, persons who have this remarkable power and faculty are not at all aware of it. This sign is known as THE LINE OF INTUITION.

Jeddu Krishnamurti is one of the most interesting figures of our present era. Discovered by Mrs. Annie Besant, widely known theosophist, who noticed that he had a very remarkable "aura" indicating spiritual gifts of the very highest orders, many of her followers were convinced that he was the long awaited "Messiah," and they resolved to give him every oportunity to perfect his "capacity" for spiritual leadership. Upon the completion of his education, Krishnamurti came to America where a large group of the Theosophists acclaimed him a "wonder youth"—the twenty-second incarnation of the Messiah who was expected some day to stir the whole world with a new message for mankind.

Page 143

LOOK AT YOUR HAND

MARIA JERITZA

HAS Fate marked you for fame? If like Maria Jeritza, celebrated opera singer, you have a circle underneath your third finger, you are very apt to become noted for some particular talent. This sign is a mark of particular success and distinction and is very often seen on the hands of singers, musicians and public speakers of note. It is called THE CIRCLE OF FAME.

Maria Jeritza was born at Brunn, Austria, and the operatic career of this beautiful prima donna has scored her the enthusiastic plaudits of two continents. Europe first thrilled to her exquisite soprano voice when she made her debut at Olmetz in 1909, and appeared at the Imperial Opera House, Vienna, in 1912, where she sang until she came to the United States. Her American debut was made at the Metropolitan Opera House, New York City, and there she repeated her Viennese successes. No fame is more coveted by singers than this. Her greatest triumphs have been in the roles of La Tosca, Fedora, Thais, Tannhauser, Die Tote Stadt, Der Rosenkavalier and Turandot, in which last Puccini opera she sang at the first New York production on November 16, 1926. She is married to the well-known Austrian nobleman, Baron von Popper. Generally, a circle is not a very favorable sign unless found at the base of the fingers. In other locations it expresses rather doubtful qualities which are increased or decreased according to the shape of the hand and the rest of the lines.

Page 144

LOOK AT YOUR HAND

RUDY VALLEE

HAVE you the gift of lyrical expression, which must find an outlet? The sign denoting this gift is a ring underneath the first finger, clearly shown in Rudy Vallee's hand and its expression may be in either music or singing. It is known as THE RING OF LYRICAL EXPRESSION.

Rudy Vallee, who, with his soft, romantic voice full of yearning and tenderness, crooned his way into the hearts of a million women, was born in Westbrook, Me. His full name is Hubert Prior Vallee. His father is of French Canadian descent and his mother was Irish. At the age of 15, during the war, he ran away from home to enlist in the navy, but was sent home on account of his age. Later he went to the University of Maine for a year and then to Yale, where he organized a college band, paying his expenses by means of his music. After his graduation he embarked on a vaudeville tour across the country. He came to New York, where he held jobs with well-known orchestra leaders and later organized his own band. One evening, while leading the orchestra, he unconsciously began to sing the chorus of a song and was greeted by so much applause that he continued to make it a practice to sing with the band. It was later, when his orchestra went on the air, that the radio audience heard his voice for the first time and feminine hearts began to fall before his romantic appeal.

ABD-EL-KRIM

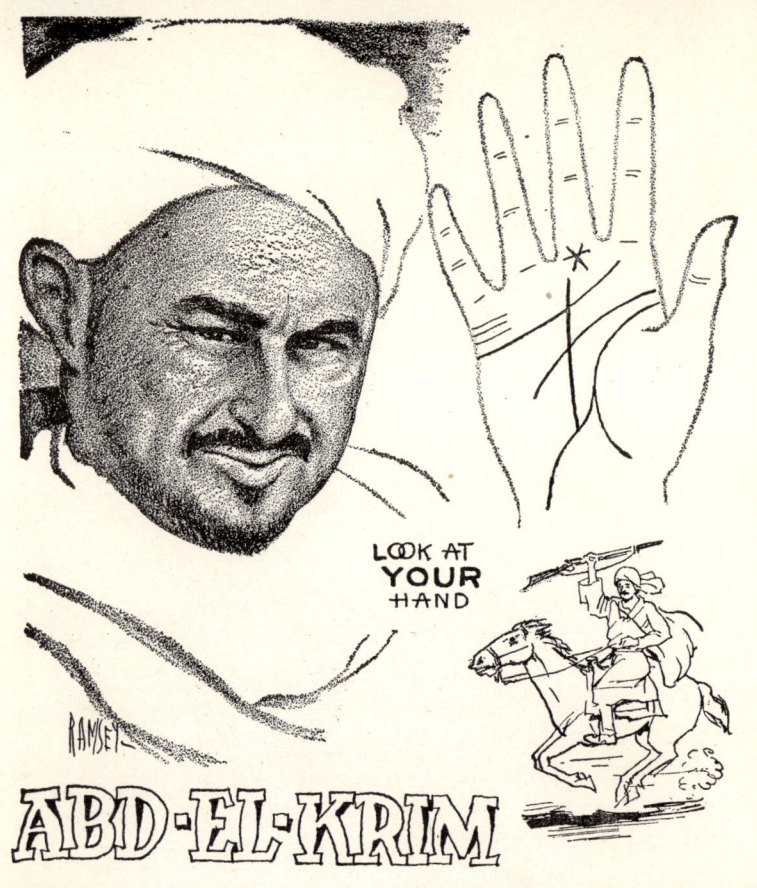

WHAT does Fate hold in store for you? Look for a star in your hand, for the star is a sign of great importance wherever it makes its appearance on the hand. With one exception, according to its position on the palm, it denotes good fortune and great distinction in life, but if found as seen on the hand of Abd-El-Krim, at the base of the second finger, it gives to its possessor a distinction to be dreaded. Such a person will be the plaything of destiny. The star in this position is known as THE STAR OF TRAGIC FATE.

Abd-El-Krim, one time master of the Riff, who held the French and Spanish armies at bay and defied every effort of modern military strategy to capture him, is now languishing in exile in a far-off French colony. Having always been an active man whose mind was fertile in a thousand schemes, just as was Napoleon's, the monotony of his present life is doubly tragic and he lives only in hope that some day the French Government may relent and permit him to go back to his native hills.

Page 146

TO RENEW CALL